IMAGES
of America

SPORTS OF
SANTA CRUZ COUNTY

In 1913, fire destroyed the original campus structure of Santa Cruz High School on Walnut Avenue. Somehow, this sweet photograph of the 1912–1913 girls basketball team escaped the inferno. Basketball was invented by Dr. James Naismith at the YMCA Training School in Springfield, Massachusetts, in 1891 and spread quickly to the West Coast, where Berkeley women tied Stanford 9-9 in 1896. It arrived at Santa Cruz High the following decade via the local YMCA, and it was a popular activity for young women until the 1950s. With the passage of the Title IX Equal Opportunity in Education Act of 1972, girls basketball returned to local high schools in the 1970s and has been a popular mainstay ever since. (Geoffrey Dunn Collection.)

ON THE COVER: The 1909 Santa Cruz Sand Crabs of the California League were managed by the legendary Bill Devereaux (fourth from left). The team, playing at what was then dubbed Casino Park, had a brutal 223-game schedule that year, and did not finish out the season, as the "outlaw" league was on the verge of financial collapse. Santa Cruz finished second in the first half, with a stellar 62-36 record, winning 17 straight games at one point. But the Sand Crabs were out of the league by July 11 due to poor gate receipts. (Santa Cruz Museum of Art and History.)

IMAGES
of America

SPORTS OF
SANTA CRUZ COUNTY

Geoffrey Dunn

ARCADIA
PUBLISHING

Published by Arcadia Publishing
Charleston, South Carolina

Printed in the United States of America

Library of Congress Control Number:

For all general information, please contact Arcadia Publishing:
Telephone 843-853-2070
Fax 843-853-0044
E-mail sales@arcadiapublishing.com
For customer service and orders:
Toll-Free 1-888-313-2665

Visit us on the Internet at www.arcadiapublishing.com

To Siri, Tess, Dylan, and Lindy

CONTENTS

ACKNOWLEDGMENTS

No one ever writes a book on his or her own. While a single name often appears on the cover, the production of a book is always a team enterprise. In the present case, many people contributed to this book over the years.

I fell in love with Santa Cruz County sports at an early age. From my Little League days nearly 50 years ago, to my son Dylan's current career in local basketball and baseball, I've been blessed with a great group of coaches, teammates, friends, and parents who have been a part of these athletic communities for nearly half a century. Space does not allow me to thank them all, but please know that the friendship, camaraderie, mentoring, and support have always been appreciated, and a lot of it went into this book.

That said, two people, Bill and Roberta Dodge, have helped me out considerably with this effort. Bill was a fixture at Santa Cruz High as a baseball and basketball coach for three decades. He and his wife, Roberta, have encouraged me to write about Santa Cruz sports history. I will always be grateful for their friendship and encouragement.

I was also blessed with two great coaches at Soquel High, Ron Walters and Tom Curtiss, who have been there for me throughout the years. I was blessed to coach the Santa Cruz High varsity baseball team in the 1990s with two of the region's great athletes and competitors, John Wilson and Rudy Escalante. Tom Wilson, Steve Seymour, Danny Braga, Joel Domhoff, Kim Joslin, Dennis Porath, Mike and Jeff Hamm, Pete Pappas (my cribbage partner), Mark Violante, Stu Walters, Kristy and Marie Netto, Paula Pappas Panelli, Gene Pini, John Sipin, Pete Newell, Tim Erwin, Bill Starrs, Angelo Ross, Kris Reyes, and Kim Luke (Mildred Fierce)—all fine local athletes and coaches—have also contributed in various ways to this book over the years. To them, I give my heartfelt gratitude.

Local historians Carolyn Swift, Phil Reader, Sandy Lydon, Stan Stevens, Frank Perry, George Ow, Joan Gilbert Martin, Barry Brown, and Kim Stoner have always been there when I needed an assist. The late Harold Van Gorder (see page 61) gifted me several of the photographs in this collection. Unless otherwise noted, all photographs are from my personal collection. Jim Seimas of the *Santa Cruz Sentinel* has done yeoman's work in keeping local sports history alive. Marla Novo and Nina Simon from the Santa Cruz Museum of Art and History have been both wonderful and thoroughly supportive.

My acquisitions editor at Arcadia, Jeff Ruetsche, has been an absolute jewel to work with. He has helped to guide this project through to the finish line. To him, I offer my eternal appreciation.

Finally, I thank my family—Siri, Tess, Dylan, and Lindy—for their love and support over the years. They've been real "sports" about this project, and I appreciate it.

INTRODUCTION

Because of its moderate and inviting climate, along with its unique blend of rugged mountains, flat coastal terraces, and welcoming beaches and surf, Santa Cruz County has always been a haven for athletic activities, dating back to pre-European contact. It remains so to this day, with a wide variety of sporting endeavors beyond the norm, from mat surfing to women's Roller Derby. Perhaps most significantly—and best known internationally—Santa Cruz served as a springboard for modern surfing. During the summer of 1885, three princes visiting from Hawaii surfed here in the Americas for the very first time.

What is not so well known is that Santa Cruz was an early bastion for organized baseball on the West Coast, beginning in the 1860s, and was home to a series of professional teams as early as the 1870s. Other colorful athletic activities took place here in the 19th century, including fire-hose teams, long-distance walking, and bicycling, along with more traditional American sporting activities, such as basketball, football, boxing, tennis, and polo. One of Santa Cruz's greatest boosters and baseball fans was the legendary local promoter Fred Swanton. During the early 1900s, he coined the promotional slogan "Santa Cruz—Never a Dull Moment." One of the reasons there was never a dull moment here was because of the plethora of sports and athletic activities going on. Swanton made sure of that.

The Santa Cruz Beach Boardwalk, which was founded by Swanton, provided an important venue for competitive swimming (the legendary Olympian Duke Kahanamoku performed here in three separate decades) along with the widely popular Plunge Carnivals and Aquatic Shows. There is also a strong tradition of women athletes in the region, in particular, Marion Hollins, the founder of Pasatiempo and one of the greatest all-around women athletes in the United States in the 20th century.

Unfortunately, most of these athletic endeavors have been largely overlooked by local historians, dating back to the late 19th century. Perhaps believing that sports and athletics are largely extraneous and incidental affairs, Santa Cruz County sports history has been largely missing from the historical record. E.S. Harrison's seminal work, *History of Santa Cruz County, California* (1892), hardly mentions a single sporting activity in the region, though many of the figures whose lives are chronicled therein actively engaged in such pursuits.

In fact, our unique sports history tells us a great deal about Santa Cruz County life, from pre-missionary times to the present. Sports are a significant cultural activity that profoundly reflect—and define—the daily life of any community. Many people identify themselves, in part, by their athletic endeavors, perhaps especially so in Santa Cruz.

In introducing this book, it is important to note what is not in these pages. The most significant omission, of course, is the absence of a chapter or two on the native peoples of this region, whose presence dates back roughly 14,000 years. This book tells its story largely through photographic imagery, so the absence of such an archive provides limitations on which stories get told and which ones do not. It should also be acknowledged that this book places emphasis on early Santa

Cruz County baseball history, and with a geographic epicenter in the city of Santa Cruz proper. I have included athletic activities from all around the county and up to the modern era—including the Santa Cruz Derby Girls and the Santa Cruz Warriors of the NBA Development League—but there is certainly room for a book of more recent Santa Cruz County sports stars and athletics.

Santa Cruz's longest athletic endearment has been with baseball, and it happens to be the number one object of my athletic affections as well. This explains, in part, why there is something of an emphasis on baseball imagery in this book. As a fourth-generation Santa Cruzan—my mother is a member of the Stagnaro fishing family on the Santa Cruz waterfront—I grew up in a community that simply loved the national pastime. The great Santa Cruz baseball player Joe Brovia—who played briefly in the major leagues for the Cincinnati Reds in the 1950s, but who had a long and fabled career in the Pacific Coast League in the years surrounding World War II—lived just down the street from me when I was a kid, and he regaled me with stories about Santa Cruz (and West Coast) baseball, lighting a fire in me that is still burning half a century later.

Whatever one's sport of choice, however, there is something for everyone in these pages. I hope the reader enjoys these stories and images from the history of Santa Cruz County sports and athletics as much as I have enjoyed putting them together. Never a dull moment, indeed.

Santa Cruz County's native people are generally referred to as the Ohlone, although they were never a tribe in the formal sense of the term. They played games and engaged the region's natural environs in a variety of ways long before the arrival of European settlers. Here, they are depicted rowing, fishing, and hunting in a 1785 illustration from *Middleton's Complete System of Geography*. (Geoffrey Dunn Collection.)

One

THE NATIONAL PASTIME

Santa Cruz has always had a love affair with baseball, dating to the 1860s, when the game was introduced on the West Coast. One of the area's first formal teams, the Olympics, played its home games in the 1870s on fields located in what is today the downtown region of Santa Cruz. By the late 19th century, baseball grew even bigger—so big that Santa Cruz was one of a handful of California cities to host a Pacific Coast League (PCL) baseball team, the West Coast equivalent of the major leagues.

There were also semipro and industrial teams scattered throughout the county—from the Felton Woodpeckers to the Watsonville Pippins to a team sponsored by the California Powder Works that played at Pogonip—all sporting strong lineups and competing more than equitably with teams from across the region and the state. Some of the players on those teams included future big leaguers like Mike Donlin, Hal Chase, and future hall of famer Harry Hooper, a teammate of Babe Ruth's who convinced the slugger to forego pitching back in his Boston Red Sox days.

Ever since, Santa Cruz has produced a steady flow of talent to The Show, including Joe Brovia, Pete Hamm, John Sipin, Dann Bilardello, Mark Eichhorn, Glenallen Hill, John Orton, Casey McGehee, Tom Urbani, Pat Burrell, Bo Hart, Robbie Erlin, as well as professional women's softball star Desarie Knipfer, and many more who pursued their diamond dreams in Santa Cruz County.

An early Santa Cruz baseball team poses in the 1890s. In the first row are the Daubenbis brothers, Ed (left) and Charles. Santa Cruz's long history of organized baseball dates to the 1860s. According to Leon Rowland's notes on file at the University of California, Santa Cruz's Special Collections: "1868: On Christmas day at 1 o'clock, p.m., there will be a Base Ball match played on Rountree's land, near new slaughter house. Those wishing to enjoy the sight are invited to be present." Another entry notes: "1871: Saturday, April 2, game 'for ball and county championship' played near racecourse. Eagles, 88; Scrubs, 45. Time: four hours."

This is perhaps the most famous baseball team in Santa Cruz County history—the 1897 and 1898 Santa Cruz Beachcombers. They were a colorful lot. The *San Francisco Call* describes them as "comedians" playing "in a nine-act comedy drama." They were also good: finishing second for the state championship in back-to-back seasons. Shown here are, from left to right, (first row) Julius Streib and Bobby Williams; (second row) Oscar Tuttle (manager), Edward Purse (mascot), and Tommy McGrath; (third row) Bill Devereaux (captain), H.E. McIntyre, J.J. Fitzgerald, Charles Daubenbis, Ed Daubenbis, Abe Arellanes, and Louis Baltz. Purse later played on African American teams and managed the Sacramento Colored Giants. He was murdered by his brother, Julius, in 1915.

One of the rarest, and earliest, photographs of a Santa Cruz–area baseball team features the Ely Electrics. This c. 1890 photograph has never before been published. The team played its games at the Vue de l'Eau Athletic Park (pictured here), located at the western end of Ely's streetcar run on West Cliff Drive. The players are wearing uniforms from some of the other teams they played on. Shown here are, from left to right, (first row) ? Draeger, Bill Devereaux, "Goldy" Goldstein, Arthur "Sandow" Otto, and Harry George; (second row) Bill Burge, ? Lindt, Embert Brown, Bobby Williams, and Tom McGrath.

Joe "Cache" Lend (left) and Rafael "Tahoe" Castro (right) were "mix-blooded" teenagers of Native Californian descent on the California Powder Works baseball team in the 1880s. According to legendary San Cruz journalist Ernest Otto (1871–1955), "Cache was a catcher and Tahoe a shortstop so fast on his feet he could almost keep up with the moving ball." In 1884, the two were arrested for arson and sent to San Quentin; they were both dead within two years of their sentencing. (Special Collections, McHenry Library, UC Santa Cruz.)

12

This rare image, also never before published, shows the Soquel Grammar School (SGS) baseball team around 1900. The players are unidentified, but it is likely that members of this squad later played on the Soquel Giants teams in the era before World War I. It is believed that the tallest player (back row, second from right) is none other than the legendary Hal Chase, who went on to star as a first baseman for the New York Yankees. Chase was raised in Soquel, where his father operated a sawmill at Cahoon's Gulch, at the juncture of Soquel and Littlejohn Creeks. (Carolyn Swift/Soquel Elementary School.)

"Turkey" Mike Donlin poses with actress Mabel Hite. This photograph is misidentified as "Santa Cruz 1898." Donlin played on the Santa Cruz Sand Crabs in 1898 and part of 1899, but he did not meet Hite until 1906. Theirs was a tragic love affair; she died of cancer in 1912. Halfway through the 1899 season, Donlin was batting .402 for the Sand Crabs when he was called up to the St. Louis Cardinals. At the time, he was also serving time in the Santa Cruz County jail for being drunk. In spite of erratic behavior, he had a lifetime big-league batting average of .333, even after taking a three-year hiatus midway through his career to try his hand at acting with Hite.

The Felton Woodpeckers pose around 1908. Baseball has always been big in the San Lorenzo Valley, with teams forming there as early as the 1870s. The Woodpeckers played their games at the south end of Felton Grove, in the present confines of Henry Cowell State Park. Shown here are, from left to right, Casey Ford (first base), Frank Silva (pitcher), Jack Piedemonte (pitcher), Howard Rubottom, Harry Trotts, Joe Piedemonte, Amos Feeley, Manuel Silvey (catcher), Martin Silvey, Bill Matting, and Bill Thompson.

Most Santa Cruzans have no idea that there was a professional baseball field, Dolphin Field, located across from the Boardwalk, at the site of what was the Casa del Rey Hotel. Games date back to the 1880s until the end of the 1909 season, when construction began on the Casa del Rey, completed in 1911. This is one of two known photographs of the interior of the ball field, showing what is believed to be a reception for the 1904 Republican State Convention. The left field foul line can be seen, right of center, extending to the outfield fence. The California Restaurant, advertised on the sign in right field, was located on Pacific Avenue. (Santa Cruz Museum of Art and History.)

Abel Joseph "Abe" Arellanes, pictured here on the Santa Cruz Electrics, was a member of a prominent baseball-playing family in Santa Cruz County that included his brothers Ed and Frank, the latter of whom played with the Boston Red Sox. Abe Arellanes, eight years older than Frank, played for several regional ball clubs, including Fresno, Watsonville, and Oakland, in addition to stints on various Santa Cruz teams. Abe was killed in 1922 while trying to intercede in a domestic dispute on behalf of his sister.

The Soquel Giants, seen here around 1907, were nicknamed the "Grover Gulch Wildcats," based on the location up Glenn Haven Road above Soquel from which most of the team members hailed. Shown here are, from left to right, (first row) Gene Dakin, Enrico "Henry" Speroni, Branch Wallace, Massimo "Max" Speroni or Avale Francesconi (a brother-in-law of John Bargetto), and Clara Jensen; (second row) unidentified, Utley Lunbeck, Howard Stoddard, and Marie Jensen. Late in his life, Paul Johnston, who was raised in Grover Gulch and played on the Giants, identified photographs with the author, but was uncertain about some identities. The ball grounds, located behind the Daubenbiss House just below Wharf Road, are still standing in Soquel. (Santa Cruz Museum of Art and History/Paul Johnston Collection.)

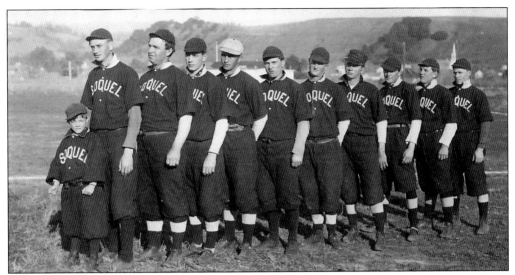

One of the most significant photographs in Santa Cruz County sports history, this image shows the Soquel Giants of 1911, featuring future hall of famer Harry Hooper (fifth from left) wearing his white Boston Red Sox cap. Posing here are, from left to right, Jack Malloch (mascot), Harvey Nugent, Clarence Angell, Milton Nugent, Hooper, Harvey Bradley, Tom Hickey, Jack Bostwick, Eugene Daken, Branch Wallace, and Paul Johnston. Visible in the background are the Soquel Congregational Church, the ridge that would later be known as Monterey Bay Heights, and the cut in the mountains that marks the Bates Creek watershed, home of the Grover Gulch Wildcats. (Santa Cruz Museum of Art and History/Paul Johnston Collection.)

This photograph, taken slightly earlier than the one above, shows the Soquel Giants sometime between 1907 and 1910. The players are, from left to right, Eugene Daken, Paul D. Johnston, Branch Wallace, Harvey Bradley, Tom Hickey, Harry Rose, Milton Nugent, Howard Stoddard, and Harvey Nugent. Johnston, the youngest player on the team, was brought up to play while in high school because of his prowess on the diamond. (Santa Cruz Museum of Art and History/Paul Johnston Collection.)

Following a game in Watsonville, Snowden's Giants player Ed Dollar sits with sisters Marie (center) and Clara Jensen around 1907. They are seen at Camp Goodall, later known as Palm Beach, located at the end of the Watsonville Railway & Navigation Company streetcar line, at what is now Sunset Beach State Park. The Jensens were the daughters of Danish and German immigrants who, according to the 1910 US Census, were farmers in Aptos. Note the baseball bat attached to Dollar's suitcase. (Santa Cruz Museum of Art and History.)

The Aptos baseball team is seen here in 1903. The players are identified on the back of the photograph as, from left to right, (first row) George Traites, unidentified, Bud Parks, unidentified, and Willie Baughauser; (second row) ? Castro, unidentified, Lloyd Haines, D.L. Maguire, ? Castro, and unidentified. (Santa Cruz Museum of Art and History.)

The Felton Woodpeckers are seen here in 1905. The players are unidentified. Many years later, a young fan recalled that "foul balls would often land in Zayante Creek. The kids were supposed to return the balls for a reward of fresh roasted peanuts, but these hide-bound shining beauties were badly needed on the old school grounds and no funds to buy them, so 'Blue Monday' wasn't always so blue . . . after a Sunday game."

The Santa Cruz Sand Crabs (or Beachcombers) baseball team poses in July 1897. Shown here are, from left to right, (first row) Charles Daubenbis, Tom McNeil (mascot), and Ed Daubenbis; (second row) Abe Arellanes, Frank Helms (manager), and Bobby "Judge Williams; (third row) William Devereaux, Julius Streib, Thomas McGrath, Charles Wilson, "Farmer" Nash, and Augustus "Bill" Burge. The Sand Crabs came in second in the state championship, losing in a final winner-take-all series to San Francisco's California Markets.

In 1907, civic leaders in smaller towns throughout the region gathered a committee to form the Coast Counties League, featuring baseball teams from Salinas, San Jose, Santa Cruz, Monterey, and Watsonville. For a brief moment, in 1913, the Pippins joined the California State League. Albert C. Leoni was a popular catcher for the Pippins in the years leading up to World War I. His grandson, Ed, was a star athlete at Mora High School and a superb sportswriter for both the *Watsonville Register-Pajaronian* and the *Santa Cruz Sentinel*.

The Pippins played their home games at Loma Vista Park in Watsonville. Here, the home team celebrates following a win against Gilroy. A newspaper clipping from 1910 lists the Pippins' starting lineup as Elmer Emerson (pitcher), Bernstein (shortstop), Mitchell (third base), Fitzgerald (left field), Nevis (right field), Thornton (first base), Marsh (center field), and Rutledge (catcher).

The Boulder Creek Saw Filers are seen here before a Fourth of July contest around 1900. The team was managed by Dan Trout. The players in this photograph are unidentified, but those who played for the Saw Filers in the early 1900s included Charley Boyce, Arthur Bowden, Johnny Hayes, Charley Wiley, Lavelle Trout, Foster McAbee, Jim Maddock, Ernie Bloom, Dick Smith, and Will Peery. Former Santa Cruz player Frank Blaidsell recalled them as "a tough, mean bunch. . . . We'd beat them at baseball and then they'd want to fight. They even threw rocks at our catcher. It got so bad that we wouldn't go to Boulder Creek anymore; we'd make them meet us on neutral ground in Felton."

One of the earliest-known images of a Santa Cruz youth team, this remarkable photograph from April 18, 1908, features paperboys for the *Santa Cruz Surf*. The *Surf* was owned and edited by the combative Arthur A. Taylor from 1880 to 1919, and many young Santa Cruz boys of that era had their first jobs peddling the paper.

This c. 1915 photograph of a Santa Cruz baseball team features former major-league pitcher Frank Julián Arellanes (second row, second from right). Arellanes, the product of an old Santa Cruz baseball-playing family, played on local teams before being called up to the Boston Red Sox in 1908, making him one of the first Latinos to play in the big leagues. In 1909, he led the league in

saves and games finished, posting a 16-12 record. Following his release from Boston, he returned to California, hurling for several teams before his untimely death at the age of 36 during the flu epidemic of 1918. (Santa Cruz Museum of Art and History.)

Without question, the greatest athlete, and sportsman of any type, to hail from Santa Cruz County was Harry Bartholomew Hooper, right fielder par excellence and team captain of the world champion Boston Red Sox in the era leading up to World War I. Born in 1887 outside of Bell Station in the southern reaches of the Santa Clara Valley, Hooper moved with his family to Capitola in 1907. After receiving an engineering degree from St. Mary's College, where he starred on the baseball team, Hooper played semipro and "outlaw" ball for teams in Soquel, Sacramento, and Alameda before being called up by the Red Sox in 1909. Selected to the National Baseball Hall of Fame in 1971, Hooper—who threw right-handed but batted left-handed—hit .300 or higher five times, stole 20 or more bases nine times, and finished among the leaders in triples seven times during his stellar career, all while leading the Red Sox to four world championships.

Hooper (second row, left) was a teammate of rookie Babe Ruth, then a pitcher (first row, right), in 1914. It was Hooper who first steered Ruth away from pitching and into an everyday role in the Red Sox outfield, where he first showed the promise that would make him the most feared home-run hitter of his generation. Ruth looked up to Hooper and viewed him as an early mentor. Later in his life, the Babe would write that Hooper was the "greatest fielding outfielder ever . . . . No doubt about it."

As was the case with most baseball players of his era, Hooper's "retirement" from the Chicago White Sox in 1925 did not put an end to his playing days. He served as a player-coach for the San Francisco Missions of the Pacific Coast League and, later, was named head baseball coach of Princeton University. In 1930, he played a season—not documented in official record books—for the Santa Cruz Padres of the California State League. In a game against Alameda, Hooper (back row, third from left) went six-for-six (not bad for a 43-year-old), and he won the league batting championship with an astounding .506 average.

Probably the most colorful athlete to play baseball in the region was William, variously "Bill," "Brick," "Red," or "Mad Dog," Devereaux, who was born in Oakland in 1871. He was a fixture in Northern California baseball from the 1890s well into the 1920s, when he was still playing sandlot ball in the East Bay. A pitcher-infielder, he started playing baseball for the Santa Cruz Electrics in the early 1890s, captained the Santa Cruz Beachcombers later in the decade, and then returned to Santa Cruz in 1908 and 1909 to serve as player-manager of the Santa Cruz Sand Crabs. Fans either loved or hated Devereaux, or, sometimes, both. Sportswriters of the day loved to take jabs at him (he was once likened to a "bottle of Tabasco sauce"), but wherever he went, he was an enthusiastic ambassador for the national pastime. He played on an American team that toured Japan, China, and the Philippines in 1908–1909.

Pictured here are the 1909 Santa Cruz Sand Crabs of the California League. The players are identified on the back of the photograph as Orth Collins, Lloyd Broadbent, Walter Dashwood, Bill Devereaux, Oscar Jones, E. Hartmann, Bill Waters, Joe Curtis, Clarence Brooks, Chester Rodgers, and Johnny Hopkins. Jones won 40 games as a pitcher that year, while Collins was called up to the Washington Senators at the end of the season. The narrow white sign above the players' heads at right reads: "Private Box for Participants—No Cards." (Santa Cruz Museum of Art and History.)

The history of so-called black baseball in the United States actually predates the Civil War. But the first nationally known professional black team was the Cuban Giants, out of Philadelphia and Washington, DC, which formed in 1885. By the 1890s, teams comprised entirely of African American players began barnstorming in the West and playing games with white teams outside the jurisdiction of organized baseball. Santa Cruz County actually had an early African American player on the Santa Cruz Olympics in the late 1870s: Joseph Smallwood Francis, a Santa Cruz High graduate and later the editor of an important African American newspaper in San Francisco, the *Western Outlook*. In the early 1900s, Santa Cruz had an all-black team called the Colored Giants, which, according to the *Santa Cruz Surf*, was "mainly made of shoe polishers about town." Players on that team included Jack Harris, the captain; catcher Louis Barry, a track star at Santa Cruz High; and a pitcher identified only as "Crubs." Floyd Berry and Robert Hunter were likely on the team.

The Coronado Colored Giants featured players from San Diego and Los Angeles. In June 1928, the Santa Cruz Padres hosted an all-black team from Los Angeles, losing 2-0 in what *Sentinel* sportswriter "Sandow" Otto called "the most colorful baseball game of the season." He described the Giants as "one of the most wonderful fielding aggregations that has ever been seen on the local pasture."

As with white semipro teams, national African American organizations often sponsored travelling black teams, most notably the Brotherhood of Sleeping Car Porters, who were more commonly known as Pullman Porters. During World War II, members of the all-black 54th Coast Artillery Regiment stationed at Lighthouse Field formed a team that played against area semipro and high school teams. Isaac Jackson, a member of the regiment and a founder of the local Missionary Baptist Church, played right field.

In the aftermath of World War I, the Santa Cruz High baseball team of 1919 was run by the Cadet Corps and Maj. W.G. Byrne. The captains were Glenn Lang and Carroll Trefts. Seen here are two of Santa Cruz's future civic leaders—*Santa Cruz Sentinel* editor and publisher Fred McPherson Jr. (standing, ninth from left); and fish magnate Malio Stagnaro (seated, far right).

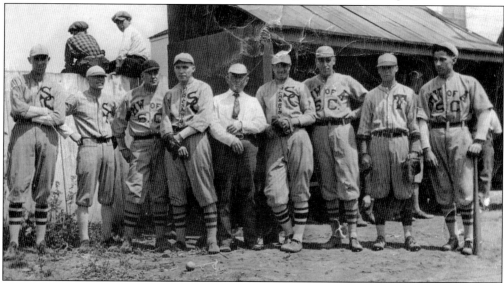

Semipro baseball became popular throughout the United States in the aftermath of World War I, as local businesses and organizations began sponsoring teams and replaced the "town" teams of an earlier generation. Pictured here in the 1920s are members of the Santa Cruz Merchants and the local order of the Modern Woodmen of America (MW of A), a fraternal benefit society founded in 1883 that provided life insurance annuities to families of deceased members. The field, known as Bush League Stadium, was located at the corner of California and Bay Streets in Santa Cruz.

Another popular local baseball team in the 1910s was the Henry Cowell Lime Burners. Shown here in 1913 are, from left to right, (first row) Amos Feeley, Manuel Silva, Edwin Wilson, and Frank Tabacchi, (second row) Harvey Bradley, Victor Trotte, Herb Manners, Albanus Sidney Theodore "Ted" Johnson (manager), Earl Jones, Fred Quirstorf, and Earl Gouin. Outfielder Frank Blaisdell (not pictured) remembered Johnson as "hotheaded and quick to get riled up." But he could also be generous. Following a 2-1 victory over the J.U. Winnegars team in San Jose, Johnson took his team out for a feast at the stately St. James Hotel. Johnson, a manager at Cowell's lime kiln operation, was later accused of stealing money from Cowell and fled the state.

In the early days of girls' sports at Santa Cruz High School, participants actually played "hardball" rather than "softball." In the 1930s, the school sported two competitive teams, the Reds and the Whites, with the Reds winning the school title in 1932. Outstanding players included Susie Caviglia (third row, fourth from left), Joyce Blake, Rene Senini, and Helen Stewart. (Esther Wilson.)

Best friends Mary Stagnaro Herman (left) and Angela "Angie" Camini Giannini pose in uniforms and with the equipment of the Santa Cruz Padres around 1928. Giannini told the author that the two young ladies had snuck into the storage room at Hughes Field and put on the uniforms as a lark. Several of Herman's grandchildren went on to become great local athletes in a variety of sports, including David and Greg Cross and Gino and Rick Rinaldi. Her great-grandson Deanne Rinaldi started as a freshman on the Harbor High varsity basketball team and is one of the top golfing prospects in the Monterey Bay Area.

The Santa Cruz Padres of 1925 played their games at Hughes Park, on the corner of Laguna and Gharkey Streets on Santa Cruz's west side. Included in the photograph here are third baseman Wilbur Ralston, pitcher Harry Martin, outfielder Harry Rodriguez, and manager Walter Cartwright. (Tom Ralston.)

The 1930 Santa Cruz High varsity baseball team was coached by the famed Clinton Earle "Doc" Felhiman (after whom the present gymnasium is named) and completed the season with a 4-3-2 mark. Players included Philip Sousa, Dario Simoni, Charlie Johnson, Dave Beaver, Domenic Lippi, Ray Carpenter, Tommy Kristinich, Lee Russell, Belden Hedgepeth, Louie Haber, and Hank Leibrandt.

Joe Brovia, "The Davenport Destroyer," signed with El Paso in the Arizona-Texas League at the age of 17. Although originally signed as a pitcher, the six-foot, four-inch Brovia led the league in hitting with a .383 average. After batting .322 the following year in the Western International League, Brovia was brought up to the PCL San Francisco Seals. He was one of the most feared hitters in PCL history and was named to the all-time PCL team. Finally, at the age of 33, after 16 years in professional baseball, Brovia got his chance at the major leagues, when the Cincinnati Reds called him up for a cup of coffee in the middle of the 1955 season.

During the 1920s and 1930s, most communities in the Monterey Bay area—Santa Cruz, Watsonville, Salinas, Monterey, Hollister, and Gilroy—hosted talented Japanese American baseball teams that played in highly competitive leagues against each other, with games scheduled on Sundays. The Santa Cruz YMA squad, shown here, includes two sets of brothers—Art, Burt, and Franklin Kithara; and Nobuyuki, Suama, Tom, and Tugio Iwanaga. The squad also includes Jim Masamori and Kuichi Takei, a crafty left-handed pitcher. Takei led the team to a championship in the Japanese Central Coast League in the late 1930s. (Janet Thelen.)

In many respects, the Japanese American leagues were similar to the more well-known Negro Leagues that flourished in the United States before Jackie Robinson broke the "color line" in 1946. In Watsonville, with a substantial Japanese American community centrally involved in the burgeoning agricultural economy of the Pajaro Valley, the Apple Giants formed in 1920s, followed by the Kasei team in the 1930s, led by Tom Mine, a left-hand-hitting outfielder and perennial .300 hitter. (Watsonville Japanese American Citizens League.)

The 1932 Santa Cruz High baseball team featured a host of players who would later go on to star on regional semipro teams—most notably the Swiss Dairy squad assembled later in the decade. Many on the 1932 squad formed the nucleus of the famed 1933 team, which went undefeated on its way to the CCAL title. Members of the 1932 team included all-league pitcher Manuel Netto, Dario Fassio, William and Barney Sinnott, Phil Sousa, Enrico Raffanti, Louis Castagnola, Livio Tamagni, and Carl Sandman.

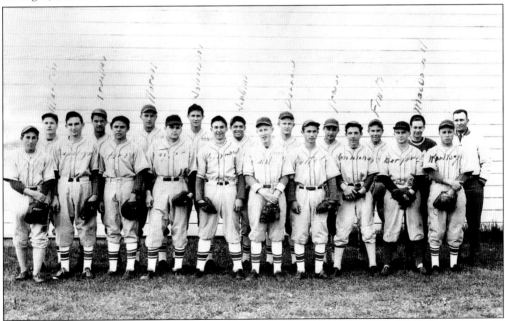

The 1945 Cardinals team featured some of the county's best athletes from the World War II era. Players included George Vomvolakis, Dick Nutter, Roy Johnson, Pete Arvelas, Kermit Darrow, Bill Casalegno, Ed Withrow, Wes Juhl, Bernard Berger, Bob Grossi, Dick Finta, and Ted Macdonnel.

During the 1940s, women's softball teams—in a "league of their own"—popped up around the country. This professional team, seen around 1948–1949, was sponsored by Fred Grellman of the Sportsman Shop and was composed of recent graduates from Santa Cruz High. Shown here are, from left to right, (first row) Lloyda Thompson, Deane Covey, Rose Lippi, Nadine Gai, and Jolene Brogden; (second row) unidentified coach, Jeanne Stagnaro Barilati, unidentified, Ann Leal, Josephine Merlotti, and unidentified coach. Barilati, a pitcher/first baseman, remembers that games were played in Salinas and Gilroy. "We did pretty well," she recalls. "We held our own." (Jeanne Stagnaro Barilati.)

Santa Cruz men's softball leagues also boomed in the era after World War II. Games were played at Cowell Park in Felton, Harvey West, and, later, at DeLaveaga Park in Santa Cruz. Lights allowed working men to play on weekday nights. The 1948 George H. Wilson softball team features, from left to right, (first row) Red Scofield, Les Marple, Bobby Soria, unidentified, and Jim Jensen; (second row) Jack Weis, unidentified, Louie Panatoni, Bobby Jackson, "Red" Slowper, and Johnny Reiss. (George H. Wilson.)

This all-star team of regional semipro hardball players in the late 1940s was dominated by members of the Swiss Dairy team, managed by Livio "Nig" Tamagni (first row, far left). Other stars on the team included Dick Fassio, Johnny Reiss, Dick Dietz, and Wes Juhl. (Carolyn Swift/Covello & Covello.)

The 1953 Santa Cruz Seahawk semipro baseball team played its games before large crowds at Harvey West Park. Shown here are, from left to right, (first row) Don Dickson, Jim Jesssen, Les Marple, Frank Ramicci, Dan Dierickson, and batboy Jack Bennett; (second row) Joe Aliberti, Fred Juhl, Bobby Jackson, Fred Sloper, and Bob Baldassar; (third row) Johnny Reiss, Ron Walters, Frank Murphy, Frank Meyers, and business manager Al Bennett.

Shown here is the 1947 Watsonville High Wildcat varsity baseball team photo from the Watsonville High School yearbook, the *Manzanita*. Pictured are, from left to right, (first row) Victorino, Sherman, Keller, Bill Dodge, Ojeda, Taylor, Robertson, and Doug Severin; (second row) Marinovich, Friermuth, Stewart, Larry Connor, Clarke, Lien, Schwenne, Wong, Petersen, and coach Emmett Geiser. Dodge and Severin went on to serve as longtime coaches in Santa Cruz City Schools. (Bill Dodge.)

Esther Frizza Wilson, widely considered to be among the best female athletes of post–World War II Santa Cruz, was named "Outstanding Athlete" at Mission Hill Junior High in 1952. At Santa Cruz High, she was a multisport competitor and, in 1955, was the recipient of the Four-Star Award, a rare honor given to young women athletes by the Girls Athletic Association. The daughter of early women's sports star Susie Caviglia Frizza, she was one of the first women named to the Santa Cruz High Sports Hall of Fame. (Wilson family.)

Until the 1958 baseball season, when the New York Giants, led by Willie Mays, moved to San Francisco, the closest major-league team to Santa Cruz County was the St. Louis Cardinals. Many local families made summertime treks to St. Louis to catch a glimpse of big-league baseball. Here, Santa Cruz Little League stars Bruce McPherson (second from left), lefty Mike Mason (third from left), and Fred McPherson (right) collect autographs from Cardinal left fielder Wally Moon. Mason once struck out 19 batters in a single Little League game; Fred had a superb career as a college quarterback; and Bruce went on to become California's secretary of state. (Mike Mason.)

The 1959 White's Mortuary Giants were coached by Pacific Coast League star Joe Brovia (back, left) and longtime civic leader Norman Benito (back, right). Members of the team are, from left to right, (first row) batboy Gary Ghidinelli (who went on to fame as a three-sport athlete at Santa Cruz High), Gary Grellman, Grant Wilson, Paul Nichols, Denis Cox, Steve Ghidinelli, Gary Castiglioni, and Tommy Martin (who died later that summer from cancer and was buried in his uniform); (second row) Bruce Hanson, Steve Welch, Randy Leonard, Nick Skorski, Danny Jasper, Johnny Craviotto, and John Morris. (Randall Leonard.)

Beginning in the late 1950s and early 1960s, the Santa Cruz County Colt League, composed of 15- and 16-year-olds, included highly competitive teams from all segments of the county. The 1963 season produced some of the best competition in league history, with the County Bank Tigers (shown here) claiming the league championship. The Tigers players are, from left to right, (first row) Pete Christensen, Pete Pini, Pete Pappas, Greg Gordon, and Bobby Scott; (second row) Bill Gilbert, Glen Griffin, Larry Oneto, Kim Joslin, and Buddy Smith. (Danny Braga.)

The 1962 Mid-County Pirates featured future Soquel High star pitcher John Pierce (front row, second from left). Other players included Gary Smith, Bob Shultz, Tom Reek, Vaughn Stumpf, Wayne Feuerhaken, Pierce, "Downtown" Danny Braga, Steve Sweat, Gary Murphy, and Gary Mashtare. Braga recalls that the following year was a little spotty for the club, with the Bucs sometimes not able to field a team. (Danny Braga.)

The 1963 San Lorenzo Valley Yankees were also a powerhouse, featuring Pete Hamm, who went on to a major-league career with the Minnesota Twins. The Yankees were coached by legendary softball pitcher Wayne Richards. Shown here are, from left to right, (first row) Dennis Bellville, Kevin Crain, Jim Smith, Dave Hall, Ed Rolle, Frank Zanotto, and Jeff Esposito; (second row) Richards, John Crain (manager), Mike Pochland, John Gho, Allan Hilton, Hamm, Larry Weide, and John Kincaid (coach). (Danny Braga.)

The Valley Sports Shop Dodgers from Watsonville featured a future major leaguer in John Sipin. Shown here are, from left to right, (first row) Ron Benich, Ben Ragsac, Steve Mine, Richard Menor, Gary Birlem, Dave Mercer, and Bob Matulich; (second row) Dick Depuy, David Welch, Paul Wilcox, Howard Knapp, Jay Kaysinger (manager), Ken Browell, Sipin, and Don Hansen. Mercer, a superb three-sport athlete, went on to a legendary coaching career at San Lorenzo Valley High School. (Danny Braga.)

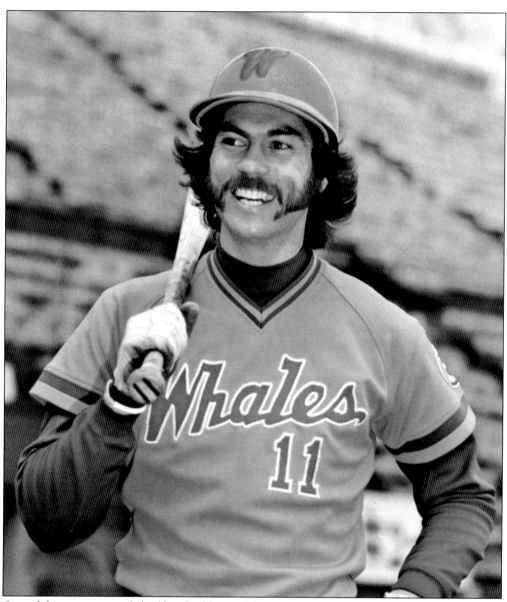

One of the most accomplished local athletes of the 1960s and 1970s was John Sipin, a two-sport star at Watsonville High in both basketball and baseball who later went on to a remarkable professional baseball career in both the United States and Japan. Sipin was the son of Johnny Imperial Sipin, a native of the Philippines, and Ethel White, a native of Arkansas. Sipin grew up playing sandlot ball in Watsonville, where his parents felt "cautious" about socializing with other parents, in spite of their son's accomplishments on the diamond. After starring in both baseball and basketball at Cabrillo College, Sipin was drafted by the St. Louis Cardinals before being traded to the San Diego Padres in 1969. In his major-league debut with the Padres, Sipin hit back-to-back triples in his first two at-bats, off left-hander Ken Holtzman. In 1972, he signed with the Taiyo Whales of the Japanese League, where he became an instant star and earned the nickname "Lion Maru" (after a Japanese cartoon superhero that morphed into a lion) because of the facial hair he sported and his fiery disposition. (Sipin family.)

In addition to being one of Japan's top hitters, Sipin was also a dynamo in the field. He became the first gaijin, or foreign-born, player to receive a Japanese Gold Glove trophy for fielding. Here he is in the 1972 Japanese All-Star Game, making a dazzling play on an errant throw, with future hall of famer Yutaka Fukumoto sliding into second base. A few plays later, Sipin threw out Fukumoto, Japan's all-time base stealer, at home on a double-steal attempt. Sipin has been named to several teams as one of Japan's all-time greatest foreign-born second basemen. He retired in 1980. (Sipin family.)

There's nothing quite like hitting a home run in front of Sadaharu Oh (No. 1), the Chinese Japanese "Babe Ruth," who holds the world professional baseball career record with 868 home runs. Here, Sipin, who was "given" to Oh's Yomiyuri Giants in 1978, is greeted by Oh and other Yomiyuri teammates at home plate after belting a *sayonara* (home run). Sipin was an offensive powerhouse in Japan, compiling a nine-year career record of 218 round-trippers and a .536 slugging percentage, along with a .297 lifetime batting average. He was named to the Japanese all-star team five times and twice received the "Best Nine" award, given annually to the best player in Japan at each position. (Sipin family.)

The 1967 Holy Cross varsity baseball team was led by Paul Bagnasco (second row, third from left), who went on to play varsity baseball at the University of Santa Clara and was drafted by the New York Mets in 1971. Shown here are, from left to right, (first row) Gary Roy, Joel Marini, Pete Williams, Charley Watkins, Rod Quartararo, and coach John Motta; (second row) Phil Schneider, Dennis Demos, Bagnasco, Gary Allyn, Tim Kelly, Mike Williams, and Gerald Malley. (Mark Violante.)

Paul Bagnasco was a three-sport star at Holy Cross and widely regarded as the best all-around athlete in the school's history. He was an all-county quarterback and was named to the *Sentinel's* all-time football team as a defensive back. Bagnasco was drafted by the Oakland Athletics following his first year at Cabrillo College and by the Mets the following year. In his first season in professional baseball, he batted .315 for the Lewiston Broncs. His former teammates still speak of him with awe and respect. Fellow Panther Terry Bernard said, "He carried us on his back." (Mark Violante.)

Regional high school baseball was extremely competitive in 1973, with four local teams battling for the Monterey Bay League northern division championship. The Harbor High Pirates, shown here, won in the end. They are, from left to right, (first row) Chuck Ryder, Boyd Herren, Gary Cutler, Paul August, John Sarmento, Tom Wilson, Erik Peterson, coach Fred Heitz, and team manger Dirk Andrews; (second row) Lance Elliot, Bob McCann, Chuck Parham, Jim Cavanaugh, Chris Ifland, Don Eggers, Ruben Rodriguez, Dan Simpson, Terry King, and head coach Claude Sharp. (Wilson family.)

The 1973 Soquel High varsity baseball team, coached by Ron Walters, tied for second place in the Monterey Bay League. Posing here are, from left to right, (first row) Ray Carillo, Brian O'Connor, Rex Nicolaisen, captain Jeff Dunn, Scott Snider, Jeff Genovese, and Mike Elrod; (second row) Dale Hendrickson, Tom Schneider, David Haley, Walters, Hugh Thorne, Jeff Hamm, and Tony Calcagno. Walters, a star on the Santa Cruz High baseball team in the early 1950s, was selected to participate in the annual California high school baseball all-star game, played at Seals Stadium in San Francisco. The Soquel High baseball field was named in his honor in 1993.

Ron Walters (center), seen here with his two eldest sons, Stu (left) and Kevin, served as the varsity baseball coach at Soquel High School from its founding in 1962 until he retired in 1975 to watch his sons play for the Aptos High Mariners. Both Walters sons were three-sport stars at Aptos, and both are inductees in the Mariner Sports Hall of Fame. Stu, a "good-glove" shortstop, went on to a stellar career as a quarterback at Chico State University, while Kevin was an all-conference catcher at Santa Clara University and played professionally with the Philadelphia Phillies organization. (Walters family.)

The Harris Brothers Togs were a top-notch semipro team that played in Santa Cruz for several years during the 1970s and 1980s. Coached by Fred Pfyffer and Dee Heren, the 1976 team included Dale Hendrickson, Greg Wehr, Larry Monroe, Ed Monroe, Jim Cavanah, Hugh Thorne, Jay Brazil, Jon Guy, Tom Wilson, Dave Munoz, and Dann Bilardello, who went on to an eight-year major-league career as a catcher with several National League teams. He hit nine home runs during his rookie season with the Cincinnati Reds.

The 1975 Santa Cruz High girls' softball team was one of the first organized girls sports teams in the aftermath of Title IX. The team went undefeated (14-0) under the guidance of coach Pete Newell. Pictured are, from left to right, (front) Leta "Yogi" Stagnaro; (first row) Elaina "Sal" Giudice, Sue "Slats" Dodge, Georgia "The Countess" Sandas, Carol "Tedo" Morgan, and Candi "Flash" Jackson; (second row) coach Pete "Gazebo" Newell, Kim "Help" Di Orio, Evonne "Goose" Sandas, and Kim "Killer" Shannon. (Leta Stagnaro.)

For a quarter of a century, youth baseball in Santa Cruz County was the domain of young boys. In the fall of 1978, Santa Cruz Girls Athletic League of Softball (GALS) was founded, commencing the following spring with its first league schedule, featuring 10 teams. One of the first was this County Bank GALS squad coached by Santa Cruz High star athlete Kathy Wilson Pappas. Players include Chris Celayeta, Shauna Schaeffer, Cathy Latocki, Cathy Rodoni, Anna Castillo, Lori Vajretti, and Kelly and Kristy Netto. (Netto family.)

No one personified Santa Cruz High athletics from the 1950s through the 1980s more than Bill Dodge, pictured here coaching the Santa Cruz High baseball team around 1978. Dodge is seen here in the third-base coaching box signaling "one out." He coached the varsity baseball and basketball teams to numerous league titles and served as a mentor, both on and off the field, to several generations of Santa Cruz athletes. In 2013, he was inducted into the California Baseball Coaches' Association's Hall of Fame. (Photograph by Bill Lovejoy.)

Bill Dodge was a star catcher on the Watsonville Wildcats 1946 baseball team. (Dodge family.)

The Santa Cruz High varsity baseball team from the early 1980s packed some serious wallop. Pictured, from left to right, are Glenallen Hill, Bill Domhoff, Dave De Esposito, Rick Munoz, Bobby Adams, Kevin Grindy, and Gino Panelli. Domhoff was a fine catcher who went on to star on the diamond at both Cabrillo College and San Francisco State. Hill went on to a superlative 13-year major-league career, belting 186 home runs and winning a World Series ring with the New York Yankees in 2000 after batting .333 and posting a slugging percentage of .735 late that season as the Yankees' designated hitter. (Domhoff family.)

The Cardinals of the early 1980s were also blessed with fine pitching. Here, John "No-No" Wilson, a crafty left-hander, toes the rubber for Santa Cruz on his way to his third year as an all-county selection. Wilson went on to a sensational collegiate career, hurling no-hitters at both Cabrillo College and San Francisco State University, where he was named an All-American after an 11-0 season in 1986. He was later inducted into the Gators' athletic hall of fame. He played professionally in the San Francisco Giants organization. (Paula Panelli.)

Santa Cruz Pony League all-stars were perennial contenders for both district and regional titles. The 1961 team was no exception. This photograph features, from left to right, (first row) Pete Pappas, Frank Moreno, Danny Braga, Bob Scott, batboy Jeff Gordon, Pete Pini, and Doug Harlow; (second row) coach Allen, John Boegel, Curt Fetty, Dave Rector, Chuck Farrar, Larry Griffin, Kim Joslin, and Gary Zabrosky. Lifelong friends Pappas and Braga went on to star at Santa Cruz High and Soquel High, respectively, before joining forces once again at Cabrillo College, along with future Watsonville police chief Terry Medina. (Danny Braga.)

The 1978 Santa Cruz Pony League champion Mets were coached by Tony (rear, left) and Eddie Torres (rear, right). Pictured here are, from left to right, (first row) Stan Prolo, Jim Woodlief, Ricky Matoza, Paul Spano, Tim Loustalot, Ricky Nash, and Jim Coffman; (second row) Mark Ripley, Kurt Boehner, Ricky Lyon, Chip Bogaard, Lloyd Rogers, John Wilson, Mike Ball, and Shawn Oliver. Wilson had a phenomenal season on the mound and at the plate for the Mets, recording an 8-1 record with a 1.25 ERA, along with a league-high .614 batting average. Loustalot went on to a professional golf career. (Wilson family.)

The Watsonville Aggies captured the imagination of local baseball fans by making runs to the national Babe Ruth World Series in 1982 and 1983. Pictured here are Aggies catcher Matt Walters (working on his glove) and talented shortstop Steve Glass, who went on to sign with the Atlanta Braves. In 1982, they played before 7,500 fans on the first night of the tournament, beating hometown favorite Denham Springs. Recalls Walters, a three-sport standout at Aptos: "We played free, relaxed, partied like rock stars and had the time of our lives." (Paula Panelli.)

For their 1983 run to the World Series, the Aggies picked up Santa Cruz High star Gino Panelli. During his senior year for the Cardinals, Panelli was named MVP of Santa Cruz County, batting .436 while compiling a 7-2 record as a pitcher. He also stole 14 bases. Panelli went 3-for-4 in the Babe Ruth regional championship game against Arizona, while picking up the win for the Aggies on the mound. (Paula Panelli.)

When asked who was the best Little Leaguer he had ever coached, former Santa Cruz Pirates manager (and Scotts Valley city manager) Chuck Comstock told the author without hesitation: Joel Domhoff. In his last season as a Pirate, Domhoff batted .750 and struck out 114 batters in 62.3 innings. He went on to be a baseball and basketball standout at Santa Cruz High—all before becoming one of the best play-by-play television and radio announcers in the region. He also developed a cutting-edge course on sports sociology at UC Santa Cruz. (Domhoff family.)

The 2010 Santa Cruz Little League champion Bolton Hill Orioles played in the District 39 Tournament of Champions. Shown here are, from left to right, (first row) Gabriel Estuesta, Calvin Dunbar, Max Wong, G.J. Hill, and Brody Murphy; (second row) Connor Rode, Nathan Katz, Marcelino Plaza, Nate Vince, Darnell White, Dylan Dunn, and Ryan Lopez; (third row) coaches Clint McCormick, Aldo Mazzei, and Richard Lopez. Mazzei had a remarkable record of either managing or coaching Santa Cruz Little League teams for more than 50 years. (Santa Cruz Little League photograph.)

The Soquel High baseball teams were always serious contenders under head coach Mitch Meyer in the 1980s through the new millennium. The 1982 squad featured future major leaguer Johnny Orton (far right). Orton, a first-round draft pick in 1987 after a superb collegiate career at Cal Poly, was a defensive specialist who played for four seasons with the California Angels. His claim to fame at the plate was doubling off Roger Clemens at Fenway Park in 1992. Also shown here are, from left to right, Jon Twaddle, Robert Olds, Tim Erwin, Bill Gibbons, and Dave Vargas. (Erwin family.)

The 1992 Santa Cruz High Cardinals varsity baseball team clawed its way to the Central Coast Section championship game, losing to Carlmont 7-2 in the title clash at San Jose Municipal Stadium. After a slow start, the team went on a run of 12 wins in 13 games. The team members are, from left to right, (first row) Jake McCormick, George Arnott, Jamie Carr, Sergio Ulloa, Chris Crawford, Neil Churchill, K.C. Kaiser, and Zach McCormick; (second row) Jason Nee, Mike Goldstein, Joel Ackernecht, Femi Ayanbadejo, Ben "Harold" Gersick, Nick Marini, Steve Cardoza, Augie Guardino, Aaron Woliczko, Mike Hendren, and Bill Yong. (Photograph by Siri Vaeth.)

One of the most dominant softball pitchers in Santa Cruz County history was Desarie Knipfer of Soquel High. She set the national single-season record for strikeouts with 518 in only 245 innings, along with a 28-6 record and a phenomenal 0.20 ERA. At one point, she pitched nine consecutive shutouts and recorded five no-hitters over an eight-game stretch in leading the Lady Knights to their first league title and the CCS semifinals in 1994. (Photograph by Dan Coyro.)

Following her legendary career at Soquel, Knipfer pitched at Cal Poly San Luis Obispo, where she was twice named Big West Conference pitcher of the year and was also a two-time All-American selection. Knipfer was named to the Cal Poly Hall of Fame in 2009. She struck out 798 batters and earned 64 wins during her four-year varsity stint. After college, she played for the Georgia Pride in the Women's Fastpitch Softball League and for the Florida Wahoos in the Women's Professional Softball League. (Don Knipfer.)

In 2002, the Aptos Little League all-stars made a celebrated run to the Little League World Series in Williamsport, Pennsylvania. They were the only local team to reach the promised land of youth baseball. They are identified on the photograph, from left to right, starting in the front, as follows: Jarred Bachan, Cesar Zermeno and Brian Godoy; Drew McCauley, Mark Lamothe and Kevin Eichhorn; J.B. Burns, Curtis Worden, and coach Andy Biancardi; Kevin Farmer, Kyle Anderson, and Tyler Raymond; coach (and former major-league pitcher) Mark Eichhorn, Andrew Biancardi, and manager Dave Anderson. (Photograph by Bill Lovejoy.)

The 2007 Santa Cruz Seals baseball team of the Palomino League won the Northern California Regional Playoffs. Managed by Buddy Carrigan (back left) and coached by Steve Peters (back right) and Mark Eichhorn (not shown), the Seals have been a dominant powerhouse for more than a decade. They are, from left to right, (first row) Tim Biederman, Beau Fraser, Adam Matulich, Andy Rogers, and Phil Incaviglia; (second row) Casey Stewart, Kevin Eichhorn, Danny Lucas, Willie Judson, Frankie Mascorra, Andrew Boggan, and Joey Parsons. Carrigan and Peters have devoted long hours to youth baseball in Santa Cruz County for nearly a quarter of a century. (Carrigan family.)

No other sibling act in the annals of Santa Cruz County sports history quite matches that of the remarkable Hamm family of Scotts Valley. All five Hamm brothers were three-sport standouts at Soquel High from the mid-1960s to the late 1970s. Pete (back row, left) was a star pitcher at Stanford before a major-league career with the Minnesota Twins; Scott (middle row, right) was a punter on Air Force's 1971 Sugar Bowl team; Jeff (middle row, left) was a starting pitcher (and teammate of future hall of famer Ozzie Smith) at Cal Poly; Mike (back row, center) was an all-league lineman as well as a hurdles and discus champion in track; Tim (back row, right) was a nationally ranked swimmer before embarking on a professional baseball career as a pitcher in the San Diego Padres organization. Sister Sandy (middle row, center), who graduated from high school in the days before Title IX, became a neonatal intensive care nurse and is married to Ken Thomas, an iconic coach and educator in Santa Cruz County. They are shown here with their mother, Dee (front row, right), and their late father, Nate Hamm, at their parents' 50th wedding anniversary. (Hamm family.)

Two

FIELDS, COURTS, TRACKS, AND RINGS

Baseball was the first organized sport to gain a foothold in Santa Cruz County, but other athletic endeavors, such as football, basketball, track and field, and boxing, soon followed. Long-distance running and walking also gained popularity in the region.

One of the most popular venues for many of these activities was the popular Vue de l'Eau Athletic Park, located near the present-day juncture of West Cliff Drive and Woodrow Avenue. The park was situated at the end of William Ely's streetcar run, and crowds often rode the trolley system out to the games and meets. Later, Memorial Field, located at the base of Santa Cruz High, served as a focal point for gridiron activity, and, even later, Harvey West Park.

The Santa Cruz Civic Auditorium eventually became the center of local basketball activity, beginning in the 1940s, with Santa Cruz City League basketball packing in crowds to watch their local heroes play in evening games before the advent of television. There were nights, according to longtime locals, when it seemed as though "everyone in town" was at the game. Hometown star Manuel Netto was at the center of City League activity for the better part of two decades. Many people consider him the most popular sports figure in Santa Cruz County history.

One of the great runs in Santa Cruz County sports history took place in 2004–2005, when the Santa Cruz High Cardinal varsity basketball team claimed the State of California Division III Championship by beating previously undefeated St. Augustine of San Diego in a come-from-behind win, 67-56, at the Arco Arena in Sacramento. It was the first state championship ever won by a Santa Cruz County team.

The 1895 Santa Cruz High football team was the most heralded gridiron squad of its era. Articles about the team were published in San Francisco newspapers. An account of a win by Santa Cruz over Union High School of Centerville notes that separate trolley cars took people wearing red and yellow, representing the school colors of both teams. In late October, Santa Cruz hosted the freshman team at Stanford University, losing in the second half 4-0. The crowd, according to one account, "made all the noise possible with throats, cowbells and horns." Players included Will Burns, Frank Armstrong, James Olive, Clarence Peck, Clyde Hawthorne, Professor Wilson (coach), Sam Faneuf, Floyd Uhden, Ralph Bias, Ralph Bachelder, James Woods, B. Stewart, and W. Barnes. (Santa Cruz Museum of Art and History.)

This 1907 photograph is the earliest known image of a Santa Cruz High girls' basketball squad. The November 1907 Santa Cruz High *Trident* notes that a committee was charged with "arranging for a new basket ball [sic] court and will be ready for use by both girls and boys." Three months later, the *Trident* reported that the girls' team was practicing at the Armory, courtesy of "Lieutenant Willey of the Naval Reserve," with games being scheduled against teams from the Business College and the YWCA. Anna Wheeler was named the captain. The team was coached by William A. Stillwell, secretary of the YMCA. (Santa Cruz Museum of Art and History.)

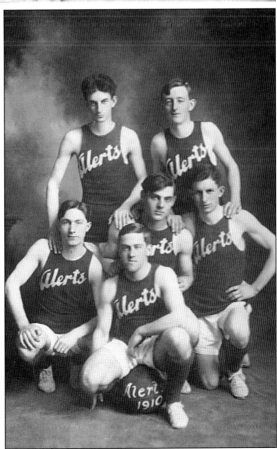

The Santa Cruz Alerts basketball team of 1910 featured top athletes from Santa Cruz High School. Shown in this photograph are C.G. Dake, Joe Costella, Hi Gosliner, Al Strong, and William "Bill" Johnson. A note on the back of the photograph indicates that Johnson, a member of the local fishing and speedboat family, "was killed at Capitola by federal gunners" over "illiset [sic] liquor." He was a notorious rumrunner during Prohibition. (Santa Cruz Museum of Art and History.)

Thomas Perrin Orchard (left) and Leo C. Smith set out for a transcontinental walk from Santa Cruz to Atlantic City, New Jersey, on June 29, 1912, before a crowd of thousands in farewell festivities at the Boardwalk. Sponsored by the *Santa Cruz Morning Sentinel*, Orchard, 23, and Smith, 19, reached Ogden, Utah, on August 2. Cards with their pictures on it were sold by the two men to raise money for their trip.

The Santa Cruz High football team of 1908 featured two African America standouts, Raymond Hunter (second row, left) and Louis Berry (second row, second from right), both of whom were multisport athletes at the high school. Other players are identified as Houghton, Hinds, Price, Hoffman, Grover, Bliss, Phillips, Archibald, and Hihn. Berry was a swift-running back for the Cardinals and would serve as captain of the 1909 squad; he is described in the yearbook as "our best man." In a game against Salinas, Hunter was accused of being a "professional" and was not allowed to participate, perhaps because he had played baseball for the Santa Cruz Colored Giants.

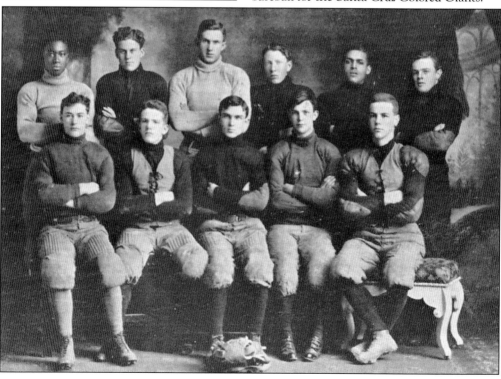

A 1919 Santa Cruz *Trident* notes that "girls' interscholastic basketball, after a long rest, has come into its own again." That squad beat King City 40-10. A year later, the *Trident* noted: "Oh, yes, the girls played basketball! They traveled with the boys most of the time and played preliminary games with the girls teams of other schools." They lost only one game, to San Jose, 22-18. By the 1922 season, Santa Cruz sported both "upper-class" and "lower-class" teams. In this image of the "lower-class" team are, from left to right, (first row) R. Gottlieb, D. Fowler, G. Cleaveland, D. Merow, H. Johnson, and G. Stratton; (second row) coach Saunders, J. Sault, V. Organ, M. Guenter, and. M. Howald. (Geoffrey Dunn Collection.)

If ever there was a gentleman athlete in Santa Cruz County, it was Harold "Gus" Van Gorder, a Santa Cruz High track and basketball star who graduated in 1921. Van Gorder seemed to be involved in almost every aspect of student life during his high school years, which were interrupted by his need to work and help support his family. He grew up to become a beloved figure in the community and an important amateur historian, writing a personal memoir entitled *Now and Then*, published in 1995. He died in 2009 at the age of 107, his remarkable memory still intact.

The 1919 Santa Cruz High School track team won the Central Coast Athletic League championship at the annual league meet in Salinas. Santa Cruz dominated the meet with 65 points, followed by Salinas with 31.5, and Watsonville with 21. Stars on the team included Irving Dake, who won the 100-yard dash; William Denton, who won the shot put and placed third in the javelin; Milton Watson, who won the 120-yard hurdles; Harold Van Gorder, who won the high jump; and Ellwood Hunter, who took third place in the 880.

Shown here is the 1919 CCAL track meet in Salinas, viewed from the grandstand. The site later became the home of the world-famous Salinas Rodeo and home to several Salinas professional and semipro baseball teams. One of the participants in the meet was John Steinbeck, the great novelist and the recipient of the Nobel Prize in Literature. In a program for the meet, he is listed as participating in the javelin and discus. One of Steinbeck's best friends at Salinas, Bill Black, won the 440 and pole vault.

This photograph was taken from the finish line. According to participant Harold Van Gorder, John Steinbeck also ran in the mile, won by Irving Harcourt Bliss (far right) of Watsonville, and in which Malio Stagnaro of Santa Cruz placed second. "When Malio crossed the finish line," Van Gorder recalled, "we swarmed him. It was terrifically exciting. Steinbeck was way behind in the pack, but none of us noticed. We were too busy circling around Malio." Van Gorder kept a detailed scrapbook of the meet, with panoramic photographs of every running contest

In the World War I era, girls' volleyball was also a very popular activity at Santa Cruz High, with squads competing both intramurally and against other schools. According to volleyball historian Phil Kaplan, the game then was played with "the bladder of a basketball."

Dubbed the "Great White Hope," retired heavyweight champion James Jeffries trained for his celebrated bout against legendary African American boxer John Arthur "Jack" Johnson at Rowardennan Redwood Park (in Ben Lomond) during the spring and summer of 1910. Newspapers from all over the world began covering his daily training activities in detail. Here, Jeffries, who had swelled to more than 300 pounds in retirement, works out with another retired heavyweight champion, "Gentleman Jim" Corbett.

James Jeffries and his large entourage arrived at Rowardennan in mid-March 1910. Pictured, from left to right, are manager "Farmer" Burns, Jeffries, main sparring partner Bob Armstrong, Roger Cornell, boxer Joe Joynski, Todd Boyer, brother Jack Jeffries, Dick Adams, Joe Samples, and "Gentleman Jim" Corbett. With a purse of $101,000 at stake (plus additional money in film rights and side bets), Jeffries and Johnson waged battle on July 4, 1910, in Reno, Nevada. In the 15th round, Johnson knocked Jeffries to the canvas. Jeffries's corner threw in the towel.

The second son of a large Portuguese farming family, Manuel "Manny" Netto was one of the most prominent—and beloved— Santa Cruz athletes in the era that spanned World War II. A 1933 graduate of Santa Cruz High School, where he starred in football, basketball, and baseball (he was an All–Central Coast League selection in all three sports), Netto went on to become a dominant force in Santa Cruz City League basketball, starring for a series of teams during an 18-year career. When he retired in 1952, a special night at the Civic Auditorium was held in his honor, and an editorial in the *Santa Cruz Sentinel* proclaimed him as "one of the finest sportsmen in local athletic" history, noting that, while he "played to win," he always "accepted defeat with dignity." (Netto family.)

Fierce competitors and longtime teammates Manuel Netto (left) and Johnny Righetti were stars on several Santa Cruz City League basketball teams together, beginning with American Legion Post No. 64, before forming a championship squad for the Santa Cruz Hotel. During World War II, Righetti served as an Army sergeant in the North African and Italian campaigns. After the war, he became a legendary restaurateur and bartender in the city, beginning at the Santa Cruz Hotel before retiring at the Sea Cloud (now Olitas), where he worked into his 90s. (Netto family.)

The 1944 White's (Mortuary) Cardinals championship Santa Cruz City League basketball team featured high school standout Roy Johnson (second row, second from left) and Manuel Netto (second row, second from right). Other stars on the team included University of Washington guard Jimmy Manion and forward Jim McDonald. (Netto family.)

Coached by the dapper Henry "Hank" Leibrandt (first row, center), the Santa Cruz Hotel 1948 Santa Cruz City League championship basketball team was considered by many to be one of the best local cage squads of all time. Players included Dick Fassio, brothers Bob and Bill Puget, Roy Johnson, the omnipotent Manuel Netto, Ernie Venturini, Hugo Armani, and Harold Sloper. (Netto family.)

During World War II, both Camp McQuaide and the Coast Guard sponsored teams that played in the Santa Cruz City League. This 1945 all-star team, selected by the editors of the Camp McQuaide newspaper, includes, from left to right, (first row) forwards John Randolph of Camp McQuaide and Paul Bailey of the Coast Guard; (second row) guard Ronnie Goodell of Camp McQuaide, center Manuel Netto of White's Mortuary, and guard Bill Jensen of the Coast Guard. (Netto family.)

The 1932 girls' soccer team at Santa Cruz High included all-stars Jeanne Panatoni, Helen Lewis, Jeanne Hayes, Yola Madciaga, Rosalie Ridella, Helen Stewart, Rene Senini, Georgia Kann, and Susie Caviglia (second row, far right). Caviglia's classmate Yolanda "Lindy" Stagnaro recalls her as "one of the best all-around girl athletes of her generation." (Esther Wilson.)

The 1949 Santa Cruz High girls' volleyball team features, from left to right, (first row) JoAnn Briggs, Josie Tabacchini, and Rose Marie Otsuki; (second row) Louise Marie Tenner, Marilla Mae Sahlman, LaVerne Anderson, Virginia Stansberry, and Ada Kasje. (Santa Cruz High Alumni Archives.)

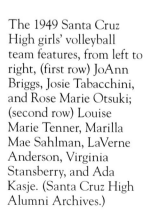

The 1941 Santa Cruz High football team was the first winning gridiron squad following several years of failure. This team, featuring several stars who would go off to fight in the Pacific and European theaters during the war, included Jack Scofield, Bob Steele, Victor Ghidinelli, Hugo Armanini, Emmet Thompson, Leo Espositio, Andy Demos, Roy Morgan, Jim Gilbert, Art Kitahara, John Davis, Bert Snyder, and the immortal Alex "Pinky" Pedemonte. Davis, Ghidinelli, Steele, and Scofield were named to the All-CCAL squad. (Santa Cruz High Alumni Archives.)

In addition to its varsity football squads, Santa Cruz High fielded competitive "lightweight" teams, preparing its younger and smaller players for the varsity. The 1944 team included Bob Tolaio, Wes Juhl, Angelo Mori, Bob Millslagle, Harry Jenkins, Way Wallach, Dick Nutter, John Amin, John Motta, Duke McCullough, and Henry Chin, who would be named to the all-league varsity squad in 1947. (Santa Cruz High Alumni Archives.)

The Santa Cruz Civic Auditorium was built as a Public Works Administration project during the New Deal. During the fall and winter months in the 1940s and 1950s, basketball was king in Santa Cruz, as the Civic hosted several city league games each week and drew steady, often capacity, crowds. Here, Ernie Pinkham of Andy's Auto Supply drives on the Santa Cruz Hotel team. (Netto family.)

The Branciforte Junior High basketball team is seen here in 1948. In the immediate aftermath of World War II, organized teams were formed at area junior high schools. Those identified in this photograph include Coach Majors, Buster Tara, Bobby Blasich, Marvin Ball, Dennis Welch, Mickey Harmon, Joe Mellow, "Fat" Hayes, Danny Patten, Leroy Morrison, Arnold Carpenter, and Fred Wagner. (Mark Wagner.)

The 1951 Class "B" Santa Cruz City League champion was Andy's Auto Supply, featuring former Watsonville High star Andy Mekis (first row, far right). Players on the championship squad are, from left to right, (first row) Del Miller, Harry Davis, and Mekis; (second row) Ben Holsey, George Wilson, Charlie Dowden, Ernie Pinkham, Ray Carpenter, and Dick O'Neil. Pinkham and Mekis were the high scorers in the championship game. (Netto family.)

While Santa Cruz City League basketball was an all-male bastion in the immediate aftermath of World War II, during the early 1950s, the league added a "girls" squad to play "preliminary" games before the main event at the Civic Auditorium. The women formed two teams, the Santa Cruz Cruzettes and a team sponsored by various concessions at the Boardwalk, including Marini's. Shown here (from both teams) are, from left to right, (first row) Joan Neilsen, Joan Brookman Stagnaro, Eva Pedemonte, Stella Ghio, Shirley Sprague, and Betty Dettle Powell; (second row) Louise Fuqua, MaryAnne Richardson, Marilyn Allen, coach Manuel Netto, Ruth Culmer, Dorothy Fulton, and Gloria Lippi. (Betty Powell.)

The women's teams played primarily against each other, though they once travelled to Fort Ord and, remembers Betty Powell, "We got rocked. They had some gals who were built like tanks." Powell recalls that coach Netto, who was brought out of retirement to coach the two squads, was "the nicest guy." When the team got shellacked at Fort Ord, he reminded everyone that "it's just a game." The league lasted for two seasons. Most of the players had been athletes at Santa Cruz High. (Betty Powell.)

Under headlines proclaiming "Glamour Added to City Cage League" for the 1952–1953 season, the *Santa Cruz Sentinel* reported that "those who have watched them in practice claim they are as expert with a basketball as they are pretty." The two women's teams wore specially tailored satin jerseys. Betty Powell remembers that the Cruzettes wore blue and white, while the Boardwalk team wore yellow. According to the *Sentinel*, they played "boys' rules." (Betty Powell.)

Mission Hill Junior High always sponsored a wide-ranging array of competitive sports for girls though the 1950s, including softball, basketball, and volleyball. Here is the ninth-grade girls' basketball champions, featuring co-captains Esther Frizza (front row, right) and Shirley Fincher (front row, left). (Wilson family.)

The Santa Cruz Seahawks are seen here in 1952. This was a legendary football team in Santa Cruz County, featuring the best gridiron players from regional high schools and, in many cases, World War II or Korean War veterans who had moved into the area. The players are center Monk D'Anna, ball carrier Jack Scofield, blocker Bob Cobb, quarterback Stu Fowler, and tailback Fred Wagner. They are playing at Harvey West Park. Signs in the background include advertisements for Stagnaro Fishing Trips, Mission Printers, Quality Paint Store, and County Bank. (Mark Wagner.)

The 1961–1962 Mora Matador basketball team was coached by the legendary Bob Bugalski, a Hall of Fame hoop star at St. Norbert College who went on to helm Watsonville High and later Cabrillo College for 14 seasons. Pictured here, from left to right, are captain James Pashiva, Mike Brautovich, Leonard Silga, Art Soto, Bugalski, Bob Winters, Phil Scurich, Jay Luich, and Duane Marsh. Seen kneeling is Ron Flores.

If his father, Manuel Netto, was a local sports icon, Phil Netto (No. 35) was not far behind. Phil was also a multisport star at Santa Cruz High, where he was best known as "Mr. Basketball." In 1956, he played in the first Dad's Club tournament held at the Civic Auditorium (fulfilling a dream of following in his father's footsteps) and was named MVP of the tournament the following year. He later starred at Hartnell and San Francisco State, before entering the Army and playing on traveling military teams. Following his Army career, Phil was a regular on the local hardwoods for nearly 50 years, until his death in 2010. The MVP award at the Dad's Club has been named in his honor. (Netto family.)

The 1955–1956 Santa Cruz High varsity basketball team included a monster roster of county athletes, many who would later become area coaches. The squad, however, had a less-than-sterling record in league play. The players are, from left to right, (first row) Jack Knight, Lou Costa, Dave Giggy, and Jerry Neuman; (second row) Leo Malaspina, Tom Curtiss, Casey Moore, Phil Netto, Bill Cleveland, Leroy Cross, and Bobby Vega. Netto finished the season with a team-high 235 points, and Cross had 196. Cross was named senior player of the year, while Netto was named to the All-CCAL team. Vega, a local sports legend, led the Santa Cruz cage team to a league title and a shot at the state championships at Berkeley in 1959.

This Holy Cross football team was led by running back Warren "Aldo" Penniman (first row, third from left). Other players included Lawrence Tomasello, Mike Sinnott, Jerry Bradford, Steve Riccabona, Charlie Elmore, Wes Price, Eldon Ross Robert Kinzie, Sandy Hicks, Dennis Abma, Fred Pino, Gus Allegri, Brian Sinnott, Denny Keith, Mike Gray, Tom Stagnaro, Bill Kelly, and Dick Piexoto. The team was coached by Rod Crump.

The 1967 Santa Cruz High Cardinals football team, one of the best of all time, went undefeated in the 1967–1968 season, with a perfect 9-0 record and a victory over Soquel in what many consider to be the greatest football game in local history. Santa Cruz won in the final 34 seconds, by a final score of 19-14 before an estimated 7,500 fans at Memorial Field in Santa Cruz. Coached by Dick Logan and quarterbacked by Kirk Waller, the team included All–Northern California lineman Walt Edwards, along with Steve Seymour, Jerry Malmin, Steve Grever, Dan Poston, Lovon "Lollie" Lowery, Tom Mitchell, Scott Stolle, Jim Sutherland, Jerry Johns, Gary Ghidinelli, Dee and Kip Herren, John Ebie, Dale Lyster, Scott Graff, Steve Agosti, Batista Bregante, and Pat Sines. (Steve Seymour.)

The 1967 Soquel High football team, coached by Dewey Tompkins, was widely considered one of the best gridiron teams of its era, even though it lost to Santa Cruz in the final game of the season. Quarterbacked by Randy Peck, the team included Gary Sakamoto, Steve Summerill, Lance and Russ Russell, Tim Jones, Carl Siebert, Chris Crabb, Russ Bethel, Steve Smiley, Jerry Newby, Lonnie Shears, Don Masters, Ernie King, Tony Fontes, Wayne Kirby, Clint Dilts, and Ted McCarroll. (Marge Peck.)

Soquel High quarterback Randy Peck sweeps around defenders from North Salinas High during his senior year, 1968. Peck was an iconic figure in Capitola and Soquel during the late 1960s. A three-sport star at Soquel High who volunteered with several youth-league teams during his teens, he won a football scholarship to the University of Utah. As the starting quarterback on the freshman squad, he led the team to an undefeated season, only to be killed in a tragic automobile accident the following spring. With an effort led by Richard Wygant, the basketball court in the Soquel High gymnasium was named in Peck's honor in 2012. (Marge Peck.)

The 1969 Holy Cross basketball team won the Catholic Athletic Association tournament before a packed house at the Santa Cruz Civic Auditorium, beating archrival Palma in the championship game. The players shown are, from left to right, (first row) Jeff Burda, Ken Lamb, and Gene Ryan; (second row) Denis Tambelini, Terry Bernard, Mike Mekis, and Tim Kelly; (third row) Phil Schneider, Gary Allyn, Phil Bargetto, and Kim Allyn. (Mark Violante..)

One of two great Soquel High basketball teams over the past half century, the Knights' 1972 squad went 14-4 in league play and 20-6 overall, dominating teams in Santa Cruz County. However, it lost twice to Alisal and was thus prevented from capturing the Monterey Bay League title. Shown are, from left to right, (first row) Jon Ditlevsen, Joe Tosta, Dave Stewart, captain Dennis Porath, and Mike Tilus; (second row) Dale Hendrickson, Don Barrett, Steve Wicht, coach Tom Curtiss, Kent Sluiter, Keith Phariss, and Kevin Phariss. Sluiter, the team's MVP, went on to a four-year varsity collegiate career at St. Mary's. (Dennis Porath.)

This 1974 photograph of the Soquel High track team features a bevy of Knight oval stars with their favorite training beverage. From left to right, are Todd Korver, Neil Theilen, Tom "Leon" Tromblee (ducking under arm), Mark Wagner, Tom Johnson, Johnnie Thomas, and Mike Hamm. Wagner still holds the Monterey Bay League meet record for the 880, with a time of 1:54:9. He won the county meet that year in the mile, 440, and 880, and anchored the final leg of Soquel's winning mile-relay team. He qualified for the California state finals in the 880. (Mark Wagner.)

The first girls' track team at Soquel High in the era of Title IX was coached by Ken Thomas. The team featured, from left to right, Kris Ostercamp, Mindy Guilbert, Sue Tompkins, and Kris Allyne. In 1977, the quartet qualified for the California Interscholastic Federation state finals in the 400-yard relay. Sprinters Laurie Spence and Leanna Mucciacciaro were also in the mix. They set school records in the 400-yard relay and the sprint medley that still stand nearly four decades later. (Gin family.)

The 1979–1980 Santa Cruz High varsity basketball team, coached by Pete Newell, featured several local sports legends. Shown are, from left to right, (first row) Kevin Ratliff, Joe Vitug, Tony Lopez, Craig Strong, John Wilson, and Shawn Kinney; (second row) Rudy Escalante, Craig Whitesell, Eddie O'Brien, Ricky Lyon, Danny Orozco, and Brian Whitesell. (Wilson family.)

"Sweet Science" promoter Jerry Hoffman produced a number of legendary boxing shows labeled "Shakedown in Quaketown" at the San Cruz Civic Auditorium in the 1990s, all to sold-out crowds. Hoffman brought in several top-notch boxers who went on to greater fame following their bouts in Santa Cruz. (Jerry Hoffman.)

"Sugar" Shane Mosley has his left arm raised in victory at a "Shakedown in Quaketown" bout at the Santa Cruz Civic Auditorium in the early 1990s. Ring announcer (and promoter) Jerry Hoffman is at right. Mosley went on to become one of the few boxers in history to claim world championships in three or more divisions, including lightweight, welterweight, and middleweight. He twice beat Oscar de la Hoya in controversial decisions. (Jerry Hoffman.)

Francis "Footloose" Farley (left) boxes at a "Shakedown in Quaketown" event at the Santa Cruz Civic Auditorium in the early 1990s. Farley began his career in karate, then switched to kickboxing, winning the North American Middleweight championship title in 1989 while recording a record of 28-2, with 17 knockouts. He later boxed successfully as a middleweight at several Shakedown events and currently runs a successful gymnasium. (Photograph by Dan Coyro; Jerry Hoffman.)

Coming into the ring at an even five feet tall and weighing 106 pounds, hometown hero Carina "La Reina" Moreno has accumulated many titles over her 15-year career, including the US National Golden Gloves crown and the USA Boxing National Championships, both in 2001. That same year, she was named Female Amateur Boxer of the Year. She compiled a 36-2 record as an amateur. As a professional, she has amassed a 23-5 record, winning the WBA flyweight crown in December 2012 in Düsseldorf, Germany, with a split decision over Suzie Kentikian. Her family runs the popular Tacos Morenos restaurant in Santa Cruz. (Jerry Hoffman.)

If there was a dominant all-around female athlete in Santa Cruz County in the 1990s, Jennifer Poli filled the bill. She was a star basketball player and track star at Soquel High, where she was an all-county selection in hoops and earned her way to the high school state championships in the long jump. Poli set school records in the 100-meter low hurdles, the 100- and 200-meter dashes, the long jump, and the high jump. She later went on to star in basketball, track, and volleyball at Cabrillo College, where she earned all-conference selections. (Photograph by Dan Coyro.)

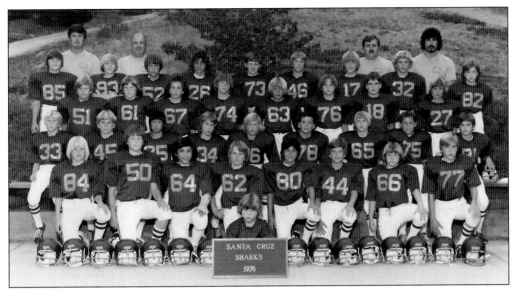

Regional Pop Warner Football, originally for boys aged 10 to 14, formed locally in 1967 with a six-team league that included the Santa Cruz Stingrays and Mid-County Mustangs. Former Santa Cruz High stars John Kirby and Fred Wagner coached the Stingrays and Mustangs, respectively. Joe Pappas served as an assistant coach of the Stingrays. In their opening season in 1976, the Santa Cruz Sharks (shown here) include John Wilson, Chip Bogaard, Gino Panelli, Anthony Ruffo, Bill Domhoff, Dave Loustalot, Jim Nicolaisen, Gary and Gavin Harvey, Gary Young, Shawn Miller, Ken Kiff, Chris Busenhart, and Kip Mihara. (Wilson family.)

Watsonville High junior Raymond Silver broke a 45-year Wildcat record (held previously by Steve Johnson of the 1968 track team) by high-jumping six feet, six inches at the DeAnza Invitation Track Meet in the spring of 2013. The five-foot, nine-inch Silver, a standout guard on the Watsonville basketball team, topped his own record the following week by jumping six feet, six and three-fourths inches at the Stanford Invitational, the first Wildcat to ever win a personal event at the prestigious meet.

The 2004–2005 Santa Cruz High Cardinal varsity basketball team claimed the State of California Division III Championship with a come-from-behind win, 67-56, at the Arco Arena in Sacramento. This photograph, taken immediately after the presentation of the trophy, includes coach Pete Newell (far right) and assistant coach Eric Manabe (far left), along with players Sean Lynch, Kevin Konopelski, Julius Freeman, Jake Pino, Austin Swift, Billy Pedersen, Jesse Lobue, Chris Sharp, Steve Hill, Cliff Sammet, Travis Haussler, Taylor Vaughn, Eric Van Vliet, Kevin Grellman, Gary Smith, Junior Russell, and Michael Norteye. The ball boy is Thatcher Sammet. Russell led all scorers in the title game with 27 points and sank a crucial three-point shot at the buzzer ending the third quarter. The championship capped a remarkable 30-year career for Newell at Santa Cruz High.

The Soquel High girls' 2004–2005 Santa Cruz County Athletic League champions and coach are, from left to right, (standing) Angel Garlepp, Kelly Gleitsman (captain), coach John Wilson, Lauren Passafuime, and Samantha Hart (captain); (kneeling) Alexis Bertlesen, Hannah Passafuime, Emily Murtha and Jordan Rocha; (front) Kanai Thomas. Hart was named MVP of the SCCAL that season. Hannah Passafuime went on to a brilliant four-year career at Brown University, where she was named to the Academic All-Ivy as a junior and earned All-Ivy honors as a senior.

Considered one of the great cage teams in Soquel High history, the 2013 champion Knights started off the season by winning the coveted Dad's Club crown, then went on to win both the SCCAL season and tournament championships. The team had a run all the way to the Northern California Division IV semifinals. Shown here are, from left to right, (first row) Tucker Wiget, Cody Valcarcel, and K.C. Snowden; (second row) Sam Walters, Tristen Hodges, Lucas Cardoza, and Jerry Levy; (third row) Scott Akrop, Dylan Hunter, head coach Stu Walters, assistant coach Tom Curtiss, Rylan Ruelli, and Nathan Vincent.

Oladele Brendon Ayanbadejo (left) and his brother Obafemi "Femi" Ayanbadejo stand on the sidelines of a Baltimore Ravens game in December 2012. Graduates of Santa Cruz High in 1995 and 1992, respectively, Brendon went on to star at UCLA and Femi at San Diego State. Excellent students academically, they followed up their collegiate performances with superb professional careers. Femi originally signed with the Minnesota Vikings and went on to win an NFL championship ring with the Ravens in Super Bowl XXXV. Brendon played for Canadian and European teams before signing with the Miami Dolphins. A three time Pro Bowl selection for special teams, Brendon also won a Super Bowl ring with the Ravens, in 2013. He has also emerged as a national advocate for gay rights and same-sex marriage. (Brendon Ayanbadejo.)

Three

FUN ON LAND AND AT SEA

So-called recreational sports, which can be every bit as competitive as the more popular team sports, have always been a big part of the sporting life in Santa Cruz County. Many of these, from surfing to beach volleyball, have their roots in the area's oceanside playground.

Two of the region's early athletic heroes were both ocean swimmers—Arthur "Red" Wallace, dubbed "The Flying Fish of the 1880s"; and W.H. Daily, considered by many to be the top swimmer in the country. Each claimed Santa Cruz as his home during the so-called Gilded Age in American history. Santa Cruzans have always blended athletic competition with their local environment.

Take, for instance, the annual Wharf to Wharf Race, dubbed "the best little road race in California," which captures the ambience of the community as it winds its way along Santa Cruz County beaches from Santa Cruz to Capitola. The race draws 15,000 entrants annually from around the world as well as thousands of visitors.

In recent years, two new entrants into Santa Cruz County sports history, the Santa Cruz Warriors of the NBA Development League and the Santa Cruz Derby Girls, have captured the imagination of local fans. Both teams play to sellout crowds at the newly constructed Kaiser Permanente Arena in downtown Santa Cruz.

The Santa Cruz Alerts championship fire-hose team, seen here around 1884, featured Samuel "Harry" Cowell, son of local limestone magnate Henry Cowell. The team regularly competed in regional and statewide competitions, winning championships throughout the 1870s and 1880s. The team members are, from left to right, Charles Edward Lilly, Cowell, Tom Witherly, John Ross, Ben Patterson, Enoch "Noch" Alzina, Charles Ogden, Elmer Dakin Jr., Con Crowley, Charles H. Dennett, John Alzina, and Frank Bartlett. Alzina later became deputy sheriff and served as a prominent baseball umpire in Central California for decades.

Watsonville sported two fire-hose teams in the 1880s—the Pajaros and the Californias. Competitions, treated as sporting events, required teams to run 400 feet, then unreel 300 feet of hose and place water on the fire. An account in the May 17, 1883, *Sacramento Union* notes that at the state firemen's tournament in Gilroy, "the Californias made a good run and got on water in 1:15." The Pajaros beat them by a quarter of a second, with a time of 1:14.75. W.R. Radcliff of Watsonville was elected recording secretary of the California Firemen's Association.

Charles Arguello Bierderman, 22, set the "coast record" in the mile at Santa Cruz, on July 4, 1887, with a time of 2:50.2, two seconds faster than the previous record. Bierderman, the scion of a longtime San Francisco family, raced throughout the state at a variety of distances in the 1880s and was one of California's top racers. Santa Cruz was a mecca of bicycle racing during this era. (Santa Cruz Museum of Art and History.)

During the 1880s, Frederick Augustus Hihn developed Capitola into a premier tourist resort, constructing the Capitola Hotel and a two-story skating rink, completed around 1884. A humorous account in the *San Jose Evening News* from the summer of 1887 notes that "visitors to the skating rink at Capitola Saturday evening were highly pleased with the efforts of C.P. Owen on the rollers. He afforded considerable entertainment by his marvelous feats. It is reported that as soon as the surgeons get through taking slivers out of him, he will be brought home on a mattress." (Santa Cruz Museum of Art and History.)

A virtually forgotten athlete in the annals of Santa Cruz County sports history, Arthur "Red" Wallace, dubbed "The Flying Fish of the 1880s," was the first person to swim 100 yards in less than a minute, for which he received international acclaim. He is celebrated as the "Champion Swimmer of California" in this tobacco trading card distributed by W.S. Kimball & Company in 1887, one of the first sport cards produced in the United States.

In a black bodysuit at left of center is legendary swimmer and swim teacher W.H. Daily, who taught lessons in Santa Cruz in the late 1870s and 1880s. In an 1881 edition of the *National Police Gazette*, Daily is proclaimed "Champion Swimmer of America." The article goes on to note Daily was willing to take on any challenger "at any distance from one to ten miles." He is described as "a wonderful swimmer and possesses great courage." The *Sacramento Union* declared that he has "no superior as a teacher." Daily was credited with saving 28 people from drowning. (Santa Cruz Museum of Art and History.)

The Boardwalk's famed Natatorium and Plunge was constructed in 1907, in the aftermath of the 1906 fire that destroyed the original casino. The Natatorium served as the premier site for indoor water activities in the region until it was torn down in 1963. The indoor pool was 144 feet long and 64 feet wide. Ocean water—pumped in from a pipe extending into Monterey Bay along the Pleasure Pier—filled the 408,000-gallon facility. The Natatorium's locker rooms could accommodate up to 2,500 visitors at any given time.

The Santa Cruz High swim team of 1922 worked out at both the beach and the Boardwalk's saltwater plunge. Swimmers here include Buzz Lent, Leo Harris (second row, third from left), Lawrence Canfield (second row, far right), Tom Hill, Jack Sault, Al O'Neil, and Jim Sowder. Harris was one of the most accomplished student-athletes in Santa Cruz High history. A championship debater, he was also the best defensive back in the CCAL and was an all-league tackle at Stanford in 1925 and 1926, playing for the legendary Pop Warner.

This photograph from the late 1880s shows rowers on the San Lorenzo River, with the Southern Pacific train trestle in the background. In summers—long before the Army Corps of Engineers constructed the current levee system in 1955—what is now known as Beach Flats often was a large tidal lagoon used for swimming and rowing. Boat rentals existed on both sides of the river. At high tides, rowers could make their way upriver all the way to the Water Street Bridge.

During the 1880s and 1890s, Santa Cruz provided a venue for encampments of the National Guard, the 1st Artillery, the 6th Infantry, and the Grand Army of the Republic, which was composed of veterans of the Union army and other military branches during the US Civil War. Boxing was a popular activity at the encampments. In 1900, a young Santa Cruz boxer named Frank Cass was killed in a "friendly" bout with Bert Whidden at the Twin Lakes summer resort. It put an end to unsanctioned bouts locally for several years.

Yacht racing began in Santa Cruz for the haut monde in the 1910s on Monterey Bay (which was often referred to by locals as "Santa Cruz Bay"), primarily during the summer months, as Santa Cruz did not have a permanent harbor until 1964. The Santa Cruz Yacht Club, organized in 1928 and which sponsors a series of annual races and regattas, is today located at the Santa Cruz Small Craft Harbor.

Two of the greatest women athletes of their respective generations, Babe Didrikson (left) and Marion Hollins (right), are featured in this photograph, taken at Pasatiempo in the early 1930s. Joining them are Johnny Lomazzi Jr. (left), son of Pasteimpo's greenskeeper, and Tommy Simmons, a four-time winner of the Pasatiempo Men's Championship. He lost the title in 1940 to 18-year-old Jackie Bariteau. In many respects, the life of Hollins, who founded and financed Pasatiempo, personifies the Jazz Age. She was as ambitious as she was talented, refusing to bow to the stultifying conventions of the era into which she was born and raised. She was one of the greatest all-around woman athletes of her time and, arguably, of the 20th century. She was a standout not only in golf, but also in tennis, steeplechase, polo, and carriage driving. Hollins was also an impassioned suffragist and advocate for women's rights. (Santa Cruz Museum of Art and History.)

In the spring of 1927, a headline appeared in the *Santa Cruz Evening News*: "Huge Development Planned by Marion Hollins Taking Shape; Clubhouse Planned." Pasatiempo was her dream come true. On opening day, September 8, 1929, Hollins (second from left) played with British amateur champion Cyril Tolley (far left), golf immortal Bobby Jones (second from right), and women's amateur champion Glenna Collett, with more than 2,000 spectators looking on. (Pasatiempo Golf Club.)

Hollins made a fortune during the 1920s investing in San Joaquin Valley oil wells, earning a reported $2.5 million. She threw lavish parties at her Pasatiempo home, hosting a steady stream of Hollywood stars and athletes, including Mary Pickford, Douglas Fairbanks, Clark Gable, Jean Harlow, Spencer Tracy, and Jack Dempsey. She is pictured here on April 8, 1934, with trainer Dick Collins (far left) and Harlow (second from left), presenting the Pasatiempo Steeplechase trophy to retired Swedish military officer Herman Flödtsrom, the rider and owner of the winning horse, Del Finnell. Hollins's luck ran out on her; she died in August 1944, alone and penniless, in a Pacific Grove nursing home. (Pasatiempo Golf Club.)

Polo was a popular sport in Santa Cruz County during the 1920s. Organized polo was originally founded locally in 1922 by Dorothy Wheeler on fields near the Wilder Ranch north of Santa Cruz. Early participants included Melvin and Deloss Wilder, Sam Leask Jr., Frank Wilson, and Dr. Golden Falconer. By the mid-1920s, the action had moved to more favorable grounds in Aptos. Here, before a match against the US Infantry of the Monterey Presidio, are, from left to right, Falconer, Wilson, Harry Hastings, and Ray Splivalo. The Polo Grounds are now a county park where soccer and baseball are played by area youth. (Santa Cruz Museum of Art and History.)

Horseback riding in Santa Cruz County has always been a popular activity. The foothills and more isolated watersheds of the Santa Cruz Mountains provide ideal conditions for casual trail riding, with stables located historically from the North Coast to the Pajaro River. In this 1936 photograph, Elvira Ghiglieri, a fabled California harpist from Stockton, and Yolanda "Lindy" Stagnaro (right), of the local fishing family, head out for a ride from the Pasatiempo Stables, owned by Marion Hollins.

Santa Cruz County stables offered both western and English riding options for its patrons. Here, Mary Pappas (left), whose family operated the popular St. Francis Grill on Beach Street, and Yolanda "Lindy" Stagnaro get ready for an English ride at the Pogonip Stables above what is now Harvey West Park.

Beach volleyball scenes began forming throughout Santa Cruz County in the 1950s. Here, southpaw Steve Slivkoff (left) spikes the ball while longtime partner Kent Kitchel (right) looks on at Capitola Beach in 1978. Future Capitola mayor Dennis Norton is about to make the dig. Capitola was a hot spot for beach volleyball, with courts first located along the Esplanade before moving closer to the wharf. Slivkoff and Kitchel were the greatest two-man team to ever come out of Santa Cruz, winning the Northern California men's beach title a remarkable 11 out of 12 years, from 1978 to 1989. (Phil Kaplan.)

The volleyball action at Sunny Cove developed in the summer of 1977, when Soquel High star Ed Morrison (left of center, in white visor and sunglasses) and some of his friends erected nets at the back of the beach. Among those in this photograph are Mike Tolaio, Mark "Wags" Wagner, Kelly Manss Ernst, Lisa Wiget, "J.D.," Michelle "Belle" Poen, "Tall" Steve, Kelly Lappin, and Jar Mellon. Robert Poen, who coordinated the Cove Invitational Coed Volleyball Tournament, is manning the desk behind the pole. "Cove Rats" staged an annual contest on the last Sunday in August for the better part of a decade. (Photograph by Wade Lindquist.)

Local beach volleyball guru Phil Kaplan spikes a ball at the Capitola four-person team championships in 1977. His teammate in the background is Leslie Jossy, with Steve Lawton (of Otter B Book fame) and Eve Zafiropoulos defending. Kaplan has taught and coached volleyball for 30 years in the community and still runs a year-round program of beach volleyball classes and tournaments called No Attitudes Allowed, focusing on the healthy aspects of competition and the development of lifelong friendships. (Phil Kaplan.)

Jeff "J.T." Tolaio spikes the ball, with his cousin and longtime teammate Lance Tolaio giving his signature "olé" gesture, during the late 1970s at Fourth Avenue Beach. The west jetty of the Santa Cruz Yacht Harbor is in background. The Tolaios were one of the top two-man teams in the region for the better part of a decade, featuring unparalleled ball control and pinpoint sets. West Coast volleyball insiders viewed them as the best two-man team "pound for pound" on California beaches. (Tolaio family archive.)

Warren "Skip" Littlefield (left), famed public relations director at the Boardwalk for nearly half a century, is seen on the Santa Cruz Pleasure Pier with his longtime friend, the legendary Hawaiian swimmer and surfer Duke Paoa Kahinu Mokoe Hulikohola Kahanamoku (1890–1968). This was Kahanamoku's third and final visit to Santa Cruz, in July 1938. Duke first arrived in July 1913, after winning the gold medal for the 100-meter freestyle at the 1912 Stockholm Olympics, and gave exhibitions in "surf riding." He set a new world record here in the 50-yard freestyle, 22.2 seconds.

In response to recommendations made by Duke Kahanamoku in 1938, Santa Cruz lifeguards were equipped with specially crafted 12-foot paddleboards for rescue operations. Shown here are, from left to right, (first row) Bill Lidderdale, Lester Eisley, and James Taylor; (second row) Elmer Geyer, Henry Ingerman, Richard Thompson, and Skip Littlefield.

Santa Cruz swimming legend Shirley Templeman also served as a lifeguard and swim instructor on the Santa Cruz waterfront. "San Lorenzo No. 2" refers to the lifeguard tower on the Santa Cruz Main Beach manned by lifeguards during the summer season. Due to currents and riptides, the Rivermouth was considered one of the most dangerous swim spots for visiting tourists unfamiliar with local waters. Templeman was one of Santa Cruz's first women surfers.

At age 16, Pleasure Point legend Jay Moriarity received international notoriety when a terrifying wipeout at the massive wave-break Mavericks was photographed by Bob Barbour and served as a cover for *Surfer* magazine. It was the biggest, most horrendous wipeout ever captured on film. Described by many as a "soul surfer," Moriarity was a well-loved and respected figure wherever he surfed. He died, tragically, in June 2001, the day before his 23rd birthday, free diving in the Indian Ocean. Shortly afterward, bumper stickers and graffiti in surf towns along the Pacific proclaimed "Live Like Jay!" (Photograph by Dan Coyro.)

Moriarity's mentor at both Pleasure Point and Maverick's was Rick "Frosty" Hesson (left), a longtime local waterman raised in the East Bay who moved to Santa Cruz in his early 20s. It was their unique and special relationship that was depicted in the superb feature film *Chasing Mavericks*, released in 2012. Hesson also wrote a memoir chronicling his life philosophy and his relationship with Moriarity, entitled *Making Mavericks* (Zola Press). His motto can be condensed to a single word: "Enjoy!" (Photograph by Bob Barbour.)

Boogie-boarding, mat-surfing, and bodysurfing are three of the biggest sports in Santa Cruz. Locals of all ages ply their skills for the thrill of a great wave horizontal to the water. Here, Santa Cruz native George Ow, who was raised in the old Santa Cruz Chinatown, cuts across a big face at Steamer Lane. A track star in his teen years at Monterey High School, Ow picked up boogie-boarding and still goes out in the water 300 days a year on the eve of his 70th birthday. (Ow family.)

Sport fishing began in Santa Cruz as early as the 1860s. Here, two anglers show a fine display of king salmon, ranging in size from 10 to 20 pounds, on what was the original Railroad Wharf, probably in the 1880s. The roof of the Neptune bathhouse and the Santa Cruz Free Museum along the Main Beach can be seen in the background.

This c. 1910 real-photo postcard of the Santa Cruz waterfront depicts visitors from Bakersfield, Oakland, and Los Angeles aboard a Faraola launch, skippered by Lorenzo Zolezzi (third from left). The catch shown here consists of 32 silver salmon weighing in at 350 pounds. The little dinghy is called the *Del Rey*. The fishermen are identified on the back of the card as "Dr. [August Francis] Schafer, Judge Creeley, C.C. Bain, H.S. Bain, and Dr. [Frederick J.] Crease."

Gladys and Ralph Giordano hold a 25-pound Pacific sea bass just off the Santa Cruz Municipal Wharf during the summer of 1941. They are standing in the *Cella Bessie*, a double-ender owned by longtime Italian fisherman Joe Loero. Ralph, who boxed professionally for 21 years under the name Young Corbett III, won the world welterweight crown in 1933 and was recognized in California as the world middleweight champion in 1938. A fierce southpaw, he retired in 1940 with a 123-11-17 record, including 33 knockouts. He was a close friend of the Stagnaro and Loero families in Santa Cruz.

From the 1930s to the 1970s, hundreds of sport fishing enthusiasts would participate in end-of-the-summer contests. The competitions were held on fishing barges embarking from the Santa Cruz Municipal Wharf. Fishermen and women from throughout the western states competed for large cash prizes. They were welcomed by large crowds and brass bands.

The Old Timers fishing competitions from the Santa Cruz Wharf produced the crowning of a king and queen annually, for the angler catching the largest fish. Here, Malio Stagnaro presents the king prize to Robbie Canepa, with the queen, Shirley Brown, looking on. Brown won the competition multiple times. Canepa, a member of an early Santa Cruz commercial fishing family, was widely considered to be one of the best regional chefs of his generation.

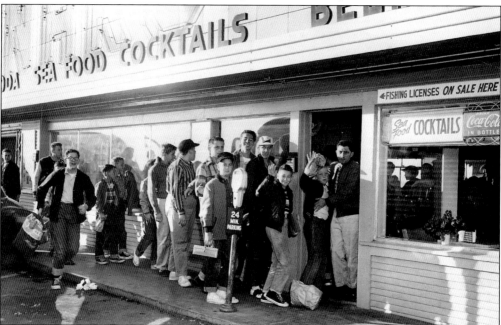

The annual contest for California paperboys gets under way at the C. Stagnaro offices in the summer of 1948. Relief boat skipper Robert "Big Boy" Stagnaro (in doorway) tries to get the young anglers ready for their day of fishing.

Long before state disability requirements, the C. Stagnaro Fishing Corporation took pride in making its vessels accessible to anglers with disabilities, particularly for military veterans returning from World War II. Here, a couple of lucky fishermen display some king salmon they caught on the party boat *Old Tom*.

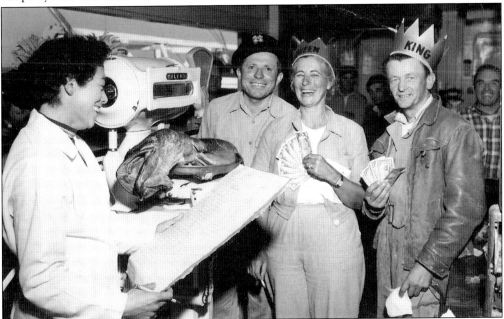

Estrella C. Stagnaro (left) was the belle of the ball at Old Timers fishing tournaments. She carefully weighed-in and documented each catch in the 1952 contest. Malio Stagnaro and Fredo Castagnola look on, while the king and queen flash their cash prizes.

Opening day of steelhead and salmon fishing in Santa Cruz was once a school holiday and an activity that drew literally thousands of anglers to area rivers and streams. Anglers would be packed in wall-to-wall. Huge steelhead and salmon runs use to make their way up the San Lorenzo River and its various tributaries annually. The runs were so thick that old-timers remember it seeming as though "you could walk across the river on their backs." Here, Leroy Cross (foreground) finds a spot in the crowd just above the San Lorenzo River train trestle in the mid-1950s. (Cross family.)

Leroy Cross was widely considered to be one of the best trout, steelhead, and salmon fishermen in the region for nearly a half century. He credits Mission Hill Junior High School physical education teacher Milo Badger with encouraging his interest in stream fishing. "I fished with him many years in my teens," says Cross. State fish and game laws restricted stream fishing to three days a week—Wednesdays, Saturdays, and Sundays. "I didn't go to school too many Wednesdays," Cross recalls. "At best, I got there at noon." (Cross family.)

Stream fishing has nearly become a thing of the past in Santa Cruz County, but in the 1800s and early 1900s, the area was known for its trout and steelhead fishing. One of the best anglers in this category in later years was Ed Morrison (left), pictured here with his sons Wes (center) and Daniel. Morrison's father, Barney, was also a premier trout and steelhead fisherman in Santa Cruz County streams. (Morrison family.)

115

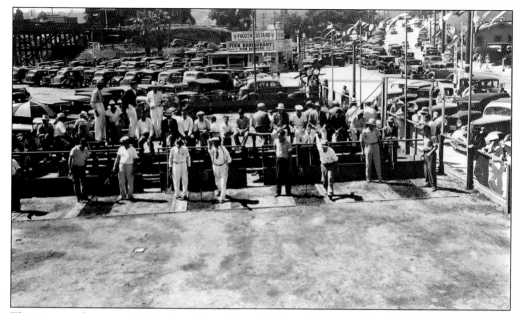

This is a rare photograph of the horseshoe pits at the Santa Cruz waterfront. The extremely popular spot was located opposite Cowell's Beach during the 1930s and into the 1950s, before the "cut" known as "Beach Hill" linked West Cliff Drive to Beach Street. This site is now a parking lot, just below the Dream Inn Hotel. The famed railroad trestle can be seen at left. The fish restaurants in the background are located on the site of today's Monterey Bay Marine Sanctuary Center.

While the earliest forms of bowling date back to Egypt and ancient Greece, bowling in Santa Cruz hit its stride in the aftermath of World War II. Photographed here is a Santa Cruz squad that traveled to Stockton for a contest on January 23, 1949. The team members are, from left to right, (first row) George Whitehead, Fred Devins, Andy Miller, Joe Parodi, "Pic" Picardo, Johnny Lamb, Irv Kalde, and Glen Snyder; (second row) Bud Ray, Heinie Waldemar, Augie Doeltz, Joe Destaillats, Joe Alveraz, George Ball, and Chris Valente.

The Santa Cruz High golf team of 1942 won the Central Coast Athletic League championship. This photograph was taken in front of the old Turner Gym. The golfers are, from left to right, (first row) Malcolm Macauly, Bill Emmons, and Willard Pennell; (second row) Robert Manildi, Robert Searle, Jim Wilson, and Dick Sauer. (Santa Cruz High Alumni Archives.)

The Santa Cruz girls' badminton team of 1946–1947 includes (not identified specifically) Sandra Macy, Jean Tucker, Jolene Brogden, and Lillian Albright. (Santa Cruz High Alumni Archives.)

Don "Mighty Bosco" Patterson was one of the most celebrated watermen in all of California—dating from his youth spent along the Santa Cruz waterfront in the aftermath of World War I, all the way to the 1960s, when he was still performing daredevil feats in the Boardwalk's plunge. A superb swimmer, diver, and acrobat, Patterson was also one of Santa Cruz's early board surfers in the 1930s and one of the most colorful figures in Santa Cruz sports history.

This is one of the few known interior images of the Pleasure Point Plunge, located just inland from Soquel Point. Originally the basement of a mansion named The Owls, built in 1914, the Plunge became a popular health spa and swimming pool in the aftermath of World War II. Refurbished by Peggy Slatter Matthews, a founder of the Capitola Begonia Festival, the Plunge offered swimming lessons taught by Pauline McNeely (who later opened the famous Polly's Puddle in Santa Cruz) and aquatics enthusiast Bob Poen. A crack in the foundation shut the pool down in 1962. (Santa Cruz Museum of Art and History.)

The DeLaveaga Golf Course, opened by the City of Santa Cruz in 1970, soon became a regular venue for business-sponsored tournaments and fundraisers. One of the most popular was the Malio's Golf Tournament, sponsored by the wharf restaurant and the C. Stagnaro Fishing Corporation, in the late 1970s and early 1980s. This foursome features, from left to right, restaurant personnel Al Fomassi, Aldo Canepa, Joe Stagnaro, and Robbie Canepa. The woman at center is unidentified.

Former professional golfer Larry Pearson (left), founder and proprietor of the landmark Santa Cruz business the Cookie Company, served as varsity golf coach at Harbor High from the late 1990s until 2001. He guided many young golfers to their first tastes of success while playing for the Pirates. At center is Harbor standout Bobby Sayus, who later starred at Cabrillo College. At right is Matt Moreno, a Santa Cruz County Athletic League MVP, who later, with his family, founded Lillian's Restaurant, on Soquel Avenue in Santa Cruz. (Pearson family.)

If ever there was someone who personified Santa Cruz County sports and sportsmanship, it is Angelo Ross. Born and raised in Santa Cruz, he was a three-sport star at Santa Cruz High and an All–Central Coast Athletic League selection in basketball. He was also salutatorian of his 1958 high school class. But it was as a coach and educator that he made his greatest impact in the region, coaching in local youth leagues and at several area high schools—including Holy Cross, Marello Prep, Santa Cruz, and Palma—all while teaching at Mission Hill Junior High for nearly four decades. (Ross family.)

The third generation of Netto athletes in Santa Cruz County, Kristy Netto was a superb basketball forward at Santa Cruz High in the mid-1980s, and later starred at Cabrillo and Bethany Colleges. She has coached the Cabrillo College women's team since 2007. Prior to that, she served as a coach for a variety of cage squads, including the Santa Cruz Special Olympics and Santa Cruz High. (Netto family.)

Ken Thomas (far right), the founding Wharf to Wharf Race director, continues to serve as official starter of the race as well as its master of ceremonies. He is also the president of the organization's board of directors. Thomas, a lifelong educator, began teaching at Soquel High in 1968 and served as a track coach there for more than a decade before becoming an administrator at various area high schools. He and Kirby Nicol (far left) have worked on the race for more than four decades. (Ken Thomas/Wharf to Wharf Race, Inc.)

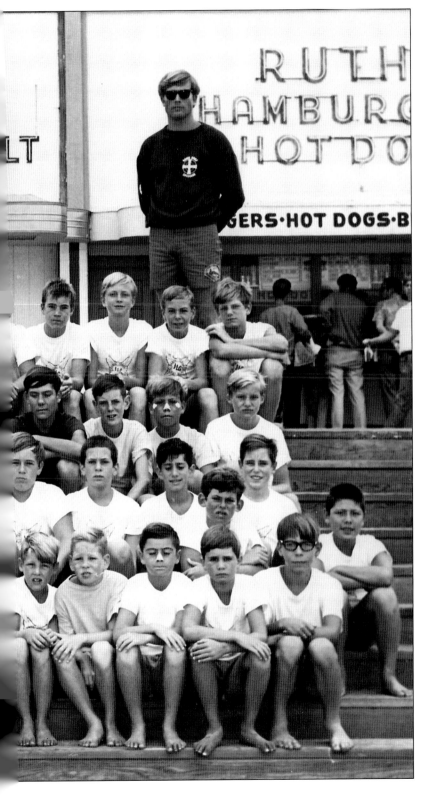

Among the most popular summertime recreational activities in Santa Cruz is the Junior Lifeguard and Little Guard program, sponsored by the city's standout parks and recreation department. The program, originally for boys, but now coed, began in the mid-1960s, with dozens of area athletes participating in its rigorous aquatic activities. Several future sports stars and community leaders participated in the 1968 program, led by instructors Kim Sundberg (top left) and Tom Brunnell (top right), including Greg Heath, Craig and Wade Lindquist, Mark Geiseke, Mark Dettle, Billy Starrs, Phil Boegel, Ken Whiting, Bruce Sundae, Rick Erlin, Dave Tambellini, Tim Tucker, Bill Mitchell, John Bagnall, Lloyd Johnson, Bill Reese, Mike Tomas, Steve Schneider, Ivan Foote, Charlie Dellamora, and four of the Malley brothers—Randall, Bruce, Russ, and Brian. (Bill Starrs.)

Four stars from Soquel High's championship girls' volleyball team pose during their amazing 2011–2012 run for the state title. They are, from left to right, middle Alex Quinn, setter Ragine Graves, libero Camille Steber, and outside hitter Bria Morgan. Coached by Kamala Sipin, the Lady Knights compiled a phenomenal 34-6 record while winning the Santa Cruz County Athletic League championship and the Central Coast Section title on their way to the Northern California championship game. Graves and Morgan were named co-MVPs of the SCCAL, while Steber and Quinn were named to the all-league team. Graves was named the *Sentinel's* Female Athlete of the Year. (Soquel High Archives.)

Tim Pappas was a two-time Northern California junior champion. In 1986, at the age of 17, he was the youngest AAA-rated player in the state. He played professionally, including in Latin America, Australia, and Europe, until his retirement in 1999. His father, Joe Pappas, was a seminal figure in local beach volleyball, helping to establish the first courts at Cowell's Beach in the late 1950s. Joe won the Santa Cruz Men's Open in 1961.

Juli Simpson Inkster, a 1978 graduate of Harbor High, has been a professional golfer on the Ladies Professional Golf Association tour for three decades, with career winnings of more than $13 million. A three-time All-American at San Jose State University, where she was inducted into the Sports Hall of Fame, Inkster has 31 tour victories, second among active LPGA players. Between 1980 and 1982, she won three successive US Women's Amateur titles. She was also a member of the victorious 1982 US Curtis Cup team. Inkster won the LPGA championship in 1999 and 2000, and the US Women's Open title in 1999 and 2002. She was voted Women's Sports Foundation Sportswoman of the Year in 1999 and was inducted into the World Golf Hall of Fame in 2000. (Inkster family.)

Widely acclaimed as "the best little road race in California," the annual Wharf to Wharf Race has become the largest summer event of its kind on the West Coast, drawing 15,000 entrants annually. Founded in 1973 by a handful of local civic leaders and track coaches—Ken Thomas, Kirby Nicol, Jim Reding, and Wayne Fontes—the original race drew 273 runners. The first medals were misspelled "Warf to Warf." By the 1980s, the race was drawing more than 17,000 participants. A limit was placed on the numbers to ensure public safety. The race now draws premier athletes from around the world and generates significant funding for scholarships and for a host of nonprofit and educational organizations throughout the community. (Ken Thomas/ Wharf to Wharf Race, Inc.)

Guided by vice president Jim Weyerman, the NBA's Golden State Warriors established a development team in Santa Cruz in 2012–2013. It quickly became one of the hottest tickets in the region. Coached by Nate Bjorkgren and led by Travis Leslie and Stefhon Hannah, the Warriors made a serious run for the NBA D-League crown. Here, Darington Hobson drives for the hoop in a playoff series against the Austin Toros. (Photograph by Chip Scheuer.)

In 2009, local women skaters formed the Santa Cruz Derby Girls as a nonprofit, all-volunteer enterprise that now holds its home games at the Kaiser Permanente Arena. The 2013 Boardwalk Bombshells include Kelly N. Marquis, Aisha Brown, Cor RaZone, Andrea "WeeZee" Lilly, Regan Eymann, Evelyn Drake, Eileen Jacinto Hill, Kaela Dilley, Terra Haddad Ma, Liv N. Letdie, Kendra "Pippi Hardsocking" Cooley, Lucero Robles, Cheri Bell, and Hollie Dilley. (Derek P. Opdyke, DPO Photography.)

DISCOVER THOUSANDS OF LOCAL HISTORY BOOKS FEATURING MILLIONS OF VINTAGE IMAGES

Arcadia Publishing, the leading local history publisher in the United States, is committed to making history accessible and meaningful through publishing books that celebrate and preserve the heritage of America's people and places.

Find more books like this at
www.arcadiapublishing.com

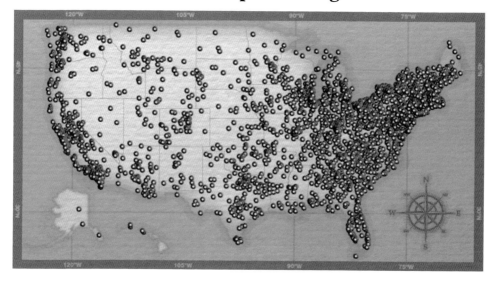

Search for your hometown history, your old stomping grounds, and even your favorite sports team.

Consistent with our mission to preserve history on a local level, this book was printed in South Carolina on American-made paper and manufactured entirely in the United States. Products carrying the accredited Forest Stewardship Council (FSC) label are printed on 100 percent FSC-certified paper.

MADE IN THE